The Pattern of Calvary

Volume I

A Paradigm Shift

JACK COCHRAN

ISBN 978-1-64140-298-9 (paperback)
ISBN 978-1-64140-299-6 (digital)

Christian Faith Publishing, Inc.
832 Park Avenue
Meadville, PA 16335
www.christianfaithpublishing.com

Printed in the United States of America

A paradigm shift is a change or revolution in the basic concepts of a scientific discipline. Thomas Kuhn said, "A scientific revolution occurs when scientists encounter anomalies that cannot be explained by the universally accepted paradigm within which scientific progress has thereto been made." The paradigm, in Kuhn's view, is not only simply the current theory, but the entire worldview in which it exists and all of the implications that come with it. This is based on features of landscape of knowledge that scientists can identify around them. A true paradigm shift is the most sudden change in perception and the point of view that anyone can experience. It is a true epiphany. Are you ready for a revolution?

My brethren, let not many of you become teachers, knowing that we shall receive a stricter judgment. (James 3:1)

Clan Cochrane

To the memory of my mother, who just months before she died woke from her hospital bed and told me she had a dream that she was reading my book. Mom, you have no idea how that carried me through some of my toughest times along this journey. Thank you for believing in me. I only wish you were here to see your dream come true. I will always love you.

PREFACE

> Have you ever had a dream Neo, that you were so sure was real . . . what if you couldn't wake up from that dream? How could you tell the real world from the dream world? (*The Matrix*)

What if what you believed to be reality was actually a dream? That reality would then be false, and the dream would be the truth. It is a nightmarish scenario that none of us would enjoy waking up to. Ultimately, though, it is our choice to wake up or remain asleep, just as it was Neo's choice to wake up and depart from that dreamworld. Unfortunately, though, religion cannot seem to wake itself up from the terrible nightmare that has descended upon it. It seems that religion, from its inception, has been caught up in some sort of illusion that has been so masterfully woven by its controllers that we as believers can no longer tell the real world from the dreamworld. What is fact and what is fiction? I can tell you from my perspective that it all appears to be fiction.

Regardless of who you are, it is impossible to escape the fact that a religious nightmare has descended upon our world. On one hand, we have radical Islam that has taken terrorism and turned it into something of a fine art to the point that we have nearly become immune to the shock value of its all too frequent bombings and beheadings. On the other hand, there's radical Christianity that never grows tired of the antigovernment taunts and graveside protests and seems to be just one eager violent step away from terrorism itself. These are the people who are all too ready to lead their devoted faithful to some remote compound or town to enslave them or, even worse, murder them in their twisted version of faith. Radicalism has hijacked the world around us and poisoned the well of faith for the rest of us who aren't willing to go along with their views of God. It's no wonder hardly any one believes in God anymore; look at what is being done in His name. I thought the message was to find the lost and lead them to a better life, not isolate and kill them?

And what of the people caught in the religious middle, the ones who are just after a normal life or the ones who want to be left alone to believe in the God of their fathers? Why are they now drifting away from the house of worship and turning to atheism or agnosticism at best? What has happened to it all? How did we get to this place of religious self-destruction? Why is it that every religion on the planet seems to be crumbling before our very eyes? Surely, there must be a reason?

Oh, sure, one could make the argument that it all looks well and good, as we see yet another megachurch going up in our community. However, underneath all the hype of their psychology-driven programs, which are supposedly drawing the masses, there still remains that unexplainable core issue of discontentment for those sitting on the pews. Even they are reporting that there is a mass exodus among their congregations. It seems that, in their attempts to grow and change with the times, they managed to turn Christianity into a mere shadow of what it once was. Their no-offense, easy-living 2.0 versions of the faith, where nothing is wrong and everything is right, have only succeeded in disintegrating the moral concept of God and church. I guess this new church isn't the soul-filling station that the masses were looking for, either. People are waking up to the fact that nothing is changing in their inner selves, though they were told it would. Every day, they find themselves looking for a god they were told existed and going out the doors of the church the same way they came in, empty and guilty.

But in reality who can blame them? If you understand the truth behind it all, you would realize that this, in many cases, is their last-ditch effort to save their faith. Like a sinking ship trying to survive the storm, they have begun to lighten the load by throwing out what they believed were all the unnecessary items of the Bible. You would think that rationality would have step in by now and said that this is not working. If that's what was truly needed, if that was the way church was supposed to be, then why isn't attendance up? Why are people still leaving? And you understand that once you let some things go, once you cast them overboard, you can never get them back. They are lost to the faith forever.

And this nightmare is not an isolated incident reserved for just one branch of religion or one particular faith. No, this phenomenon, this falling away, has infected both large and small, from the old-school Southern Baptist to the modern-day Methodist. It is a tangible collapse of faith that has begun to spread everywhere. It's like a religious pandemic has crept into the farthest reaches of the body and infected every organ with its symptoms of doubt and disbelief, killing off the weak and making sick the once proud faithful. And what of our doctor, the Great Physician? Wasn't He the one who was supposed to have the cure for all of this? It's as if He has left the building, and no one was notified. At least with Elvis, we knew when he left. But if that's the case, if He is gone, then can anyone tell us where He went or if He will, if ever, return?

But I suppose if there was a root cause to this collapse, it would be in large part due to the fact that the nanny states that were created by the churches of old have all but dissolved; their spell of control has been broken by a world of rebellious youth and information, and many are finding they don't want what is left. The reality of the masses losing their confidence in religion's ability to cure them from their illness has begun to set in; in fact, they are beginning to wonder if it was ever there at all. And if history has taught us anything, it's that when one controlling power collapses and there is not another one there to fill it right away, a vacuum is created. And since nature abhors a vacuum, she is often forced to fill it with something far worse than what was there before; in our case, she's filled it with such things as radicalism, atheism, and agnosticism. These ideas have filled the spiritual vacuum in the hearts and the minds of the believers that were intended for God to fill. All of this has dealt a tremendous blow to the confidence and morale of the still faithful. It must be hard to stay faithful to a god from which the entire world seems to be departing.

Even these faithful ones are beginning to find out that our crumbling houses of worship have a growing void of any real experience with God. Which has left them wondering, what kept their parents there all that time? Was it blind obedience or a pledge to loftier ideal of morality? Did they stay because it was the right thing to do, or did they stay because God once resided there? Is it possible that religion does not have all the answers? Is there even a god? It has been an awful long time since anyone has seen or felt Him. But despite the feelings of doubt and unbelief assailing their consciences, they managed to keep trudging along, going because there's really nowhere else for them to turn. The church truly is the only one offering that freedom from a guilty conscience and a chance at an eternal life.

But then that's the million-dollar question, isn't it? If not there, then where? How do you find that illusive freedom that your soul is screaming for in these kinds of circumstances, especially when all you hear are the same old clichés like "everyone sins a little every day" and "those aren't addictions, you're a mature Christian, you can handle them?" And if those don't work, they break out the really big sedative: "You have fallen into a pool of grace and you can't get out, so it really doesn't matter what you do—God forgives you."

Religion has unknowingly created a logic trap for the conscience of the believer by blurring the lines between right and wrong. This has left the faithful with this unshakable feeling of being trapped. On one hand, they are hearing that they are all right and that everything is okay. But in the back of those cliché-pounded minds, they know something is not right. They know something is missing because they are experiencing a contradiction in terms and feelings. They catch themselves saying, "If I'm okay, then why do I still feel guilty?"

And it is not that they don't believe in God's ability to relieve their conscience. If they didn't, they wouldn't be there. They just don't believe in that god. And how could you believe in a god that turns a blind eye to every immoral act a person does? Where has the god of those like Charles Finney and Jonathan Edwards gone? What do you think they would say if they were to show up today?

Furthermore, how does one even restore such a faith when there are some 33,000 plus versions of Christianity alone, spread over some 238 countries, all of which are claiming that they are the only way to God? They can't all be right, can they? No, that spokes in a wheel all going to a single-hub philosophy do not hold water, especially when you have the founder Himself saying, "Enter by the *narrow gate*; for **wide** is the gate and **broad** is the way that leads to destruction, and there are **many** who go in by it. Because narrow is the gate and difficult is the way which leads to life, and there are few who find it" (Matthew 7:13–14).

So then, where do you begin? How do you find your way through a religious maze where everyone is right and everyone else is wrong? I mean, really, 33,000 roads to God? I guess by that standard, Jim Jones was just another way, right? If that's the case, then let's all drink the punch and go home.

But really, what's the faithful to do? They sense a trap, but can't quite define it because they can't place their eyes on it. You can't fight what you can't see, right? Yet one thing is for sure about those of the faith. They may not know how they got there, or how to get out, but they know that this is not it—This is not the dream of Jesus Christ. We were never meant to feel trapped by religion, but liberated. The intent was never to have the faith fractured into so many pieces that the hopeful could never put it all together; but it was always intended to be one faith, as the Apostle Paul so plainly declared to the Ephesians, "There is **one** body and **one** Spirit, just as you were called in **one** hope of your calling; **one** Lord, **one faith**, **one** baptism; **one** God and Father of all, who is above all, and through all, and in you all."

We all came in looking for that unity; we came in with the notion that once you became a follower of Jesus Christ, the guilty conscience and the problems of this life would be gone. That's what they promised us, right? The power to be freed from our chains. They promised us a change, but they delivered none. But who can you really blame? Religion? God because He allowed it to become this way? Surely not God, but it does leave one wondering if this God we believe in really cares that we are caught up in this trap. Or even worse, is religion just some cruel joke made up by man to control the masses and to take advantage of the hopeful? Regardless of the blame, it is the faithful who find themselves left with only one of two options: leave the church like so many are or stay and keep trying to convince themselves that they really have a relationship with a god they cannot feel.

The Beginning

What if I told you that I felt and experienced those same issues, and that same something in the back of my mind kept telling me that all was not right? For some unexplained reason, the logical connections between what they were telling me about God and what I was feeling just weren't being made, but I couldn't explain why. I just knew that there was more substance and depth to my questions than the answers I was getting. The best analogy I could give you was that it was like showing someone an old black-and-white photo and then trying to convince them that there was color there. I could see the images and the descriptions, but the colors weren't coming into the picture.

Something was missing. Don't ask me how I knew, but I just did. My mind kept telling me that something was off, and maybe, that's because there were just too many unanswered questions to things I felt they should have the answers for. But instead of ignoring those feelings like so many before me, I began to search for what it was. I knew the answer was out there, and I knew that it would find me if I wanted it to. I have since come to realize that the desire for truth must be present if you are ever going to find the answers. The question of why truly does drive us, but oftentimes, it is never where we think and rarely where we want to go. Truth can be quite terrifying at times.

I knew there was a way out of the trap; I just had to find it. In hindsight, I guess what set me apart from everyone else was the fact that there was a natural questioning of authority in me. They assumed I was going to be like everyone else and just accept their explanations for what they were and move on or that I was going to be impressed with their in-depth explanation of nothing. What they did not, or could not understand, was that I'm not like everyone else. I didn't spend my childhood sitting on church pews or in a *Leave It To Beaver* family. I grew up sitting on bar stools, surrounded by drugs and violence. I grew up with conmen and crooks as my role models, taking my life cues from one of the most bizarre families you could ever imagine. Normal was something that lived next door. So mind you, the day that I walked through the back doors of any church for something other than a funeral or a wedding would be a huge step for me. I was like everyone else who comes into church for the first time. I came in looking for help. I had finally reached the end of my rope with the status quo, and I knew something had to change, and change fast or I was going to end up dead.

So, naturally, when I came in, I had questions like all of us, but that criminal mind was not as trusting as most. It wouldn't let me just blindly follow, no matter how hard I tried to override it. When I fell from the high of conversion, I realized that, as much as I wanted to change, I would never totally be like them. The questions I had were entirely different from theirs; and, for the first time, I realized that I'm not wired like everyone else; I see things differently. In that moment of self-revelation, I discovered that there were several side effects left over from that former life.

For one, I found that I was void of certain boundaries because I lived outside of them for so long. Where most people saw rules and lines that could not be crossed, I saw places that need to be crossed. I saw the lines and beyond as vast unexplored gray areas. What some might have called a curse, I began to realize was a gift; it allowed me the liberty to question and to touch things and ideas that weren't supposed to be touched. That was the very thing that would lead me to the truth. The other side effect was that I still possessed the ability to read people. I had spent my whole life around criminals and their scams and had learned how to spot a con. It was second nature. I knew when someone was telling me the truth, and unfortunately, most of what I was seeing in religion was a con.

That was the very thing that drove me to seek out the truth about the Bible; not only did I need to prove to myself that this was real, but also I wanted to prove it to others that not all of religion was a Jim Bakker con. I knew the answers were in the unexplained. There was a reason why I had those questions and those feelings, and I knew that I was not the only one. Mind you, it wasn't God that I had the problem with; it was with the people who said they were His chosen, the ones that were supposed to be looking after the flock. I knew that there was a way back for all of us; I just had to find it.

The quest

So the search began, and I soon realized that when you start out on a quest of discovery, you are not really sure what you are going to encounter. You just get a direction, and you go. After a while, the quest takes on a life of its own, drawing you deeper into its mysteries. I had no idea what I would find, but I knew that when I found it, all of my questions about God and the Bible would be answered. So instead of suppressing my natural criminal way of thinking, I just let it run loose like a wolf in the sheepfold of the Bible. I began to question everything that modern religion was telling me because I knew something was missing and that something was pushing me to go and find it. After all, it's my soul we're talking about here. Shouldn't I be allowed to question? Shouldn't I be allowed to cross those lines of thinking and not just accept the unexplainable as just having faith? As *The X-Files* so famously put it, "The truth is out there," somewhere.

And that's just what I found out there in that ethereal somewhere of the Bible, lying dormant between the lines and pages; I found its long-forgotten truths. But like Neo in his moment of rehabilitation when he asks Morpheus, "Why do my eyes hurt?" We find that he is answered with the unsettling truth, "You've never used them before." Like Neo, I was blinded by the revelation of reality. I was seeing what I had never seen before, and my mind was going in directions it had never gone. It was like seeing the Bible for the first time, but with complete understanding, unclouded by opinions or ideals. I was seeing it for the first time in its purest form, the way it was always intended to be seen; and with each turn of the page, it began to blow to pieces all of our long-held beliefs and concepts of the Bible. The flood of emotions it released was almost uncontainable, and I knew at that moment that the eyes of the world had to be opened as well. They needed to know the truth about the Bible and where we really stand with religion. Somewhere in our past, we lost this truth; and when that happened, it all stopped being about God and started being more about man's agendas. This is why the whole world is so frustrated with religion and why people are leaving churches in droves and becoming atheists. It's because religion has lost the truth of the Bible and has given up on the core message.

The Purpose

This book will not only explain what that message is but also answer all those hard questions that we have all had about the Bible. It is intended to challenge everything you have ever known about it, crossing lines and boundaries that will certainly offend some and even enrage others. Its main intent, though, is not to damage, but to enlighten. Unfortunately, truth has a way of doing that to people, doesn't it? As the saying goes, "truth hurts," and it certainly will here. Not everyone embraces the truth, even though it is the very thing that Jesus said He came for: "For this cause I have come into the world, that I should bear witness to the truth. Everyone who is of the truth hears my voice" (John 18:37).

Ironically, truth would be that very thing that would get Him killed. Truth is why the prophets were slain and tortured; truth is what set Martin Luther on the run after he posted "The 95 Theses" and subsequently changed the face of religion. Truth is why Tyndale was burned at the stake. Who would have ever imagined that truth would be a capital offense?

It seems truth in every instance has set the world on fire and changed the course of history. You would think that men would rejoice in the truth; but, in reality, they hide from it because it exposes their true nature. Man would rather live in his dreamworld. But then that's the beauty of truth, isn't it? It is like a double-edged sword, where one edge cuts and injures, mortally wounding those in its path, and the other edge gives life and liberty. As Jesus said, "You shall know the truth, and the truth will set you free" (John 8:32). And that's all I'm offering you here: truth—nothing more, nothing less. I'm not here to twist the Bible; that's been done enough. However that does beg the age-old question as Pilate so profoundly and simply put it, "What is truth?" Good question. Read the book, and you be the judge.

So I imagine at this point you're feeling a bit like Alice, tumbling down the rabbit hole of thoughts. If that is true, then let me ask you a question: Are you someone who accepts the current state of religion because you're expecting to wake up from this nightmare? Ironically, at this moment, that would not be far from the truth. Do you believe in fate, Neo? If not, why? Is it because you don't like the idea that you're not in control of your life? Believe me; I know exactly how you feel, because I always thought I was in control of my life until I woke up.

Can I suggest then why you're here, and why you feel compelled to read this book? You want to read this book because you know something, but what you know, you cannot explain—You only feel it. You have felt your entire life like there is something wrong, not just with the world, but with religion. You cannot explain it, and you don't know what it is; but it's there, like a splinter in your mind, driving your very soul mad. You can't really describe what's wrong and you can't quite put your finger on it, but you know it's there. It is the very thing that makes you question your faith; it's that unsettling feeling that keeps you up at night worrying about your eternity, and it has plagued you your entire Christian walk. You know what I'm talking about, don't you?

Do you want to know what it is? It is the illusion of freedom, and it is everywhere; it's all around you even now, in the very room you are in. You see it when you look out your window or when you turn on your television. You can feel it when you go to work, when you go to church, or when you kneel down beside your bed to pray. It is the religious world that has been pulled over your eyes to blind you from the truth. What truth? That you're still a slave, like everyone else in this world. You were born into bondage, born into a prison that you cannot smell, taste, or touch. You were born into a prison, not only for your mind but also for your very soul.

Modern religion has sold us a false bill of goods; it told us we were free, when in reality, we've remained in slavery. It has kept us trapped in this illusion it calls freedom. It is a web of deception that people all over the world are plugged into, having their very life force drained from them by a religious machine that keeps them trapped in the construct they call freedom. This is the real-life *Matrix*. Like the machines of *The Matrix*, it has sold the masses this illusion of freedom from bondage they so desired; but, in reality, it was only a façade, a deception designed to keep them in captivity and drain them. There has been a fundamental breakdown in the truth of the Bible, and those thinking they have been set free are, in fact, still in bondage. It is the worst kind of bondage: the kind where one thinks they are free, but, in reality, they cannot see, smell, or touch the prison they are in. Unfortunately, I cannot tell you what this illusion is—You must be shown.

So, this would be your *Matrix* "red pill, blue pill" moment. Take the blue pill and put the book down, go home, and live your life and believe what you want to believe. Take the red pill, though, and stay in wonderland; and I'll show you how deep the rabbit hole goes. I'll show you what has been either hidden from us or lost and just how far off course we really are with God. I'll take you to that place in the Bible where everything you thought was reality becomes an illusion, and the illusion becomes the reality. It's time to stop trying to convince yourself you have a relationship with God; it's time to wake up! Remember, that's all I'm offering you is the truth, nothing more.

All great truths begin as blasphemies. (George Bernard Shaw)

INTRODUCTION

> A beginning is the time for taking the most deli-
> cate care that the balances are correct. (Dune)

We all seek balance. In our personal lives, in our careers, and especially in our spiritual lives, regardless of the path, we look for balance
in it. Perhaps that is why Christianity is so out of control now, as it
never really struck a balance with the Old Testament. In our modern
Christian lives, it seems that the amount of time spent on studying
and expounding on the New Testament far outweighs the Old. This
has caused an imbalance not only in our understanding of Christ and
Calvary but also in our spiritual lives.

In my studies, I have found that there is nothing more intriguing
or more difficult for people to understand than the Old Testament
scriptures and the reason they were inspired by God in such a way.
And yes, I said by God, because many people today believe that the
Bible is an invention of man and that it was devised to enslave one's
natural passions and to create control through guilt. But in reality,
what god would want to make his creation feel guilty? I believe the
number one reason people do not believe the Bible is God-inspired is
because religion has simply failed to give a proper explanation. Time
and time again, they have offered up lame explanations to some
legitimate questions to people who are not stupid. Not everyone is
a blind follower. Accepting the unexplained as "just having faith" is
not going to cut it for them. The whole world has seen where that
got the followers of Jim Jones and David Koresh. So what are they to
think when the very man of God can't explain the whys of the Bible?

Because, believe it or not, there is a natural curiosity in man to want to know everything they can about God; and when that curiosity is not, or cannot be, satisfied, one begins to discount God as being real; they can't see how a God of significant love and power could ever orchestrate such a complicated book. This ultimately prompts phrases from people like "the Bible was written by men, and it's full of mistakes and contradictions," and to a degree, that is true. It was indeed written by men, but there are no mistakes or contradictions residing between the covers. It is, for lack of a better word, perfect; and by the end of this book, you will also say the same thing.

You see, the Bible wasn't just written by men to chronicle the lives and history of the Jewish people as some believe, and it was much more than having the Law of Moses and the prophets before the Israelites as a guide. The Bible was compiled and inspired by God, firstly, to prove that He is the creator and the only God; secondly, to prophesy or foretell the coming of His Christ; and finally, to illuminate the path for mankind back to its former relationship with their Creator. So if we discount the Old Testament as something that has been done away with by Christ and unnecessary, which it was not, we would be discounting a literal treasure trove of information; it is the origin of our faith and the very thing that Calvary was built on. So how can we just dismiss those first thirty-nine books as merely a collection of endless genealogies and laws that have no bearing on our modern walk with God? The simple answer is we can't, but without understanding the Old, we will never see how the two are so inexplicitly intertwined.

Now, I suppose the major reason that the majority of us do not grasp the Old Testament is because we did not grow up in Orthodox Judaism. You understand that the Christians and the Islamists are the latecomers to the party; the Jews have had an additional two thousand years with the scriptures, which puts them at an extreme advantage over the rest of us, as the Apostle Paul said, "What advantage then has the Jew, or what is the profit of circumcision? Much in every way! Chiefly because to them were committed the oracles of God" (Romans 3:1–2)

Every day, from the time they woke up until they went to bed, they ate, drank, and lived the Old Testament, just as they do today; it literally became a part of their religious genetic makeup. So we, as non-Jews, have been playing catch-up the whole time; the only advantage that we have for the time being is that they have, in part, been blinded by God for our advantage, again as Paul said, "For I do not desire, brethren, that you should be ignorant of this mystery, lest you should be wise in your own opinion, that **blindness in part** has happened to Israel until the fullness of the Gentiles has come in" (Romans 11:25–26).

But, again, that time gap has worked to our disadvantage because we have never really had the time to fully assimilate the Old Testament; and without the proper teaching of these old systems, the founders of this new faith could only come away with a very literal understanding of it, especially seeing that the Gentiles had all just recently come from worshiping pagan gods. So without this being pounded into their minds as it was the Jews, they would naturally struggle. But, to be fair, even the Jews had a hard time decoding the complex allegorical meanings of the Old Testament scriptures; otherwise, they would have known that it was the Christ that had come.

Even the great Apostle Paul struggled with making those connections between the Old Testament scriptures and what was now taking place with Jesus and this new movement. In fact, it was such a challenge to him that, after his conversion, he exiled himself to the Arabian Desert for some three years to sort out the details, as he wrote, "But when it pleased God, who separated me from my mother's womb and called me through His grace, to reveal His Son in me, that I might preach Him among the Gentiles, I **did not** immediately confer with flesh and blood, nor did I go up to Jerusalem to those who were apostles before me; but **I went to Arabia**, and returned again to Damascus. Then after **three years** I went up to Jerusalem to see Peter, and remained with him fifteen days."

So if Paul, who by his own account was a "Pharisee of Pharisees," struggled with it, then how could these newly converted Gentiles ever come to an understanding of such a complex system in such a short amount of time? It would be natural to forsake the Old

Testament scriptures for a new simpler way that promised freedom from the complexity and rigidity of that old system. Why use the Old Testament when the letters of Paul and the apostles would suffice? And who can blame them? The Old Testament was written in a highly complex allegorical code that only the very few have ever gotten a glimpse of. Yet to discount the importance of them or to ignore their connections to the New Testament would be foolishness on our part.

These allegories were written to be our examples. According to the Apostle Paul, "Now these things (in the Old Testament) were our examples, to the intent we should not lust after evil things, as they also lusted" (1 Corinthians 10:6). The Old Testament was to be a guide for us to follow, both morally and spiritually, all the way to Calvary, and to identify the Christ when He came. But, dare I say, many of us have discarded it, feeling that Christ has destroyed the old ways. This is an impossibility because Jesus Himself said, "For verily I say unto you, **Till heaven and earth pass away**, one jot or one tittle shall in no wise **pass from the law**, till all be fulfilled" (Matthew 5:18).

So seeing that there is still some relevance to them and that they were intended to be a guide for us to follow, why wouldn't we place more importance on understanding them? It was even by those Old Testament scriptures that God said that He would establish the basis for biblical knowledge and doctrine, as Isaiah had written, "Who shall he (God) teach **knowledge**? And whom shall he make to understand the **doctrine**? Them that are weaned from the milk, and drawn from the breast? For precept must be upon precept, precept upon precept; line upon line, line upon line; here a little and there a little" (Isaiah 28:9–10).

Now, in case you don't know what doctrine is, it is by definition "a condensing of beliefs or a body of teachings or instructions that are taught as principles or positions to guide, they are the essence of teachings in a given branch of knowledge or belief system, i.e. Christianity."[1] So, in our case, doctrine is the condensing of the

---

[1]   World IQ.

Bible's teachings into formative rules and guidelines for man to follow; and, thankfully, God taught Isaiah how to construct those rules and guidelines into solid Biblical doctrines and beliefs.

It is done by compiling enough precepts together to form a general understanding of the message that God is transmitting to us. What are precepts? They are commands or principles that are intended as a general rule of action, which is a principle or regulation governing conduct, action, procedure, or arrangement, that is, the Law of Moses. The other aspect to creating doctrine was to compile the lines. What are lines? They are the verses of scriptures, such as the ones above, that are compiled together to form those precepts. So, by compiling the lines, we form our precepts, and the precepts form our rules or doctrines that govern the Bible. Easy, right?

And let me point out here that building a doctrine is not the taking of one single line or verse to form a rule like so many have done, but it is using many lines to form those precepts. So the overriding message here is that, without a doctrine in place, the Bible would become aimless in directing the lost back to the Creator. It would be like living in a city with no laws; only chaos and disorder would rule, which is the primary cause of Christianity's splintering into those 33,000 plus pieces. No one can agree on what is, and what is not, important.

It seems that, somewhere along the way, we have forgotten how to follow the rules. God put them there to guide us, not divide us; however, without an understanding of how the Old overlaps the New, the only outcome is division. So precept must be upon precept and line must be upon line to prevent such things from occurring.

Now the unspoken rule when forming Biblical rules or precepts is that you need at least three examples or lines to form a general rule. By doing so, one begins to form a solid scriptural doctrine by getting information from several different Bible locations: "Here a little and there a little." So if something is said or done once, then no, it cannot be used to create a rule; twice, then maybe; three times, and now you have enough examples to form a precept. It is known as the codification or the arranging of the verses in a systematic way to form our rules; this process is the foundational principle of making a law or code. And so it is on this principle of building lines and precepts that I would like to establish the basis for what you are about to read in the context of this book. It is a step-by-step formulation of the doctrine of Calvary through a systematic arranging and compiling of the scriptures, not only to display the true meaning of the Bible but also to make my case against religion and their current position. By compiling so much information, I hope to remove any doubt that this is the original intent of the Bible.

And please keep in mind that this is not the sort of book that is intended to tear down the Bible or religion by claiming that someone has found some lost scripture or scroll, revealing so-called truths about Jesus, such as He had a wife and some kids or that He sinned just as we do. No, all such claims are nonsensical in the scope of the Bible. If He did do those things, then He was not the Christ; I don't expect you to understand that right now; but, by the end, you will. No, the intent is to put us back on course, and I intend to do so by using the Bible and related materials, and I will also use it to prove that God and His Christ are in fact very real.

Now in this book, we will be following the three main "types and shadows" that form the basis for the symbolic construction of Calvary, as well as the allegories that are designed around these events. And when I say Calvary, I am speaking of a condensing of those three events surrounding the last days of the Christ, which were the death, the burial, and the resurrection. Understand that it did not all take place on that day or location per se, but again, I'm just compressing the three events into one phrase to simplify our understanding. As for those who either are new to the Bible or do not know some of these terms, let me briefly describe to you just what types, shadows, and allegories are.

Types, Shadows, and Allegories

Now, a Biblical shadow is a faint hint of what is to come. It is an indistinct image or an idea conveyed through symbols or persons; it is the act of intimating or implying; it is making known something indirectly. A good example would be from the writer of Hebrews when he wrote, "For the law, having a **shadow** of the good things to come and not the **very image** of those things, can never, with those sacrifices which they offered continually year by year, make those who come unto it perfect" (Hebrews 10:1).

What the writer was implying by this verse is that the law was just a shadow of the Christ to come, but not the very image of Him, for if it could do what Christ did, then there would be no need for Him to come and sacrifice Himself. Shadows also incorporate the use of people as well, such as Joseph, Moses, and Jonah, which we will get to further in the book.

Now, a type is slightly different from a shadow; it is, as the Scofield New Reference Bible puts it, "a divinely purposed illustration of some truth. It may be: (1) a person; (2) an event; (3) a thing; (4) an institution; or (5) a ceremony. Types occur most frequently in the Pentateuch, but are found, more sparingly, elsewhere. The antitype, or fulfillment of the type, is found generally in the New Testament." Types basically set the standard in one of those five areas, be it animal sacrifice, such as a spotless lamb, or in the form of persons, like Adam, Abraham, and Moses, and events such as the flood or the Red Sea crossing; and they go as far as delving into institutions such as the Sabbath or the priesthood.

Types are used along with shadows, patterns, and allegories not only to foreshadow coming things such as the Christ but also to reveal God's intent for humanity and uncover hidden Biblical truths. These are equally equated by God into the general scope of prophecy as the direct written prophecies themselves are, and they aid in binding the Old Testament to the New Testament. Nearly everything we will cover in this book will fall under one of these two tools and certainly under all five of those areas. As for the antitypes, the fulfillment of these types, and shadows, they will be displayed when necessary.

And lastly, we have my favorite, the allegory that is as Dr. Wheeler puts it, "as a literary device, in its most general sense is an extended metaphor. Writers or speakers typically use allegories as literary devices or as rhetorical devices to convey hidden meanings through symbolic figures, actions, imagery, and or events, which together create the moral, spiritual, or political meaning the author wishes to convey. The allegory readily illustrates complex ideas and concepts in ways that are comprehensible to its, readers, or listeners." I love the allegory because of its complex nature. In order for us to understand the message it is transmitting, one must first read the entire story and then process the meaning. Allegories reveal the deeper hidden truths of the Bible, which are almost always concerning the Christ and Calvary, such as the Passover.

The Pattern

Now, when we place these types and shadows together along with the allegories, they begin to from the definite patterns of Calvary, which is again the death, the burial, and the resurrection of Jesus Christ. By revealing these three patterns in various forms, I will show you that Calvary was the sole concept upon which God constructed the entire Bible. As the Apostle John wrote, "And all that dwell upon the earth shall worship him, whose names are not written in the book of life of the **Lamb slain from the foundation of the world**" (Revelation 13:8). Christ and Calvary were on God's mind even before He created the earth and before Moses ever wrote the first word.

So, it will be upon these three themes that all of our focus will be, and we will follow these reoccurring patterns from Genesis to Revelation. When we are done, it will be quite plain that the Bible was built on these foundations. I wish I could just tell you what it is; that would save you and me both the time. Unfortunately, though, most people are not accepting of plain truth; they must be shown in order to be convinced, and that often requires a lot of explanation. Coming to an understanding of Biblical concepts is kind of like looking at those magic eye puzzles that are generated by computers. At first, they look like a bunch of gibberish for your eyes; but if you follow the instructions, your eyes become attuned, and a 3-D image suddenly appears out of the pages. That's how the pattern of Calvary works—It trains your mind to see the pattern.

It is the process by which we make sense of the Bible—placing it and its patterns in categories that are definable and understandable. Without instruction on what things mean, the Bible becomes just a collection of stories and rules that make no sense to the average reader. And that shouldn't be so because people truly want to know what the Bible means. There is that natural curiosity in man to want to know his Creator. We are like abandoned children wanting to find their biological parents; there's just an unexplainable drive in us to discover.

So without proper instructions on how to navigate the Bible, most people are left frustrated and confused. They often walk away from it more confused than when they started. They didn't know what to look for; they were never taught how to focus their vision. With the proper training, though, anyone can focus on the pages and watch the patterns appear in the form of stories and events, people, and objects. Once you become attuned to it, when you know what to look for, the Bible takes on a new life, and you will never see it the same way again. It will be with you forever, as the process is irreversible.

So as we approach this understanding together, you'll begin to see that this book is written more like a repair manual than a narrative. I did it that way because you need to see the interworking of the Bible and how it was designed. Consider this a manual for tearing down and rebuilding the engine of the Bible, with the end result being a true running and active salvation. It's truly the only way most of us are ever going to understand what's going on inside the Bible because, for most people, just reading the Bible and viewing it from the outside leave you with too many questions. It's kind of like opening the hood of your car—you see all the gadgets and gizmos, but you don't know how it all works. You just know that you put gas in it and it goes; and if it breaks, you're stuck; but if you know how it works, it empowers you to fix the car and get moving.

This book is designed to get you inside of the inner workings of the Bible and explain to you what each part is and how it functions. When we are done, you will be a sort of master mechanic of the Bible. By doing this, you will begin to understand how God's patterns are relevant to you and your salvation. The Bible is just like an engine: It can only work one way. So if you take the time to understand and see how the pattern works, you'll understand how the Bible works. It is my desire to put us all on the same level of understanding because, in that moment, you will see that my opening statements are not unfounded or outlandish, but, instead, based in fact.

Christians can no longer argue from the standpoint that it was an experience that changed their lives. Most people are not having that spiritual experience; and for those that do, it becomes as Voddie Baucham said, "An argument that anyone could drive a Mack truck through." People have life-changing experiences every day in any number of faiths. Take Voddie's favorite example, Malcolm X. Though he grew up the son of a Baptist lay speaker, it was his encounter with Islam while in prison that changed his life, not Christianity. Malcolm's experience and conversion literally made history. So why didn't Christianity work for him? Where did it fail and Islam succeed? Possibly because Islam appealed to him at that moment in time; but, again, it was an experience, one that he later detracted from which cost him his life. So then did the experience make Islam right? No, but all too often, I hear people tell me that "I live this way because of the experience I had with God"; and that's probably true; but that argument is not valid if you're trying to make the case that Jesus Christ is the only way or that your religion is the only way to be saved.

The time has come for us to go beyond just the experience. So who is right if the path is as narrow as Jesus said? It can't be 33,000 lanes wide, right? No, it can't, especially when you see the pattern and understand just what God has intended for man. The pattern will narrow the lanes and shatter most of our former concepts we have about the Bible. The time has come for us to stop dealing only in the experience and start dealing in facts about the Bible and our salvation; we can no longer justify the unexplainable as just having faith. It's time to unmuddy the waters of religion and truly find out just what God expects of us.

And that's not always a bad thing. At this particular point in time, it seems we are all spiritually bankrupt in one way or another, regardless of what faith you belong to. Sometimes, there needs to be a fresh start, but that can't happen until the old structure is torn down and cleared away to build anew. As the historian Chester Starr once said, and I loosely quote, but he said that sometimes, the old structures can no longer move along the lines then apparent, they need something to come along and turbulently shake the foundations so that nothing of the old way stands, thereby leaving room for the new to arise.

But where do we begin? How do we purify this pool of knowledge? I suppose at the beginning. It is the only logical place to start. First, though, let me take you to my beginnings, to the things that unlocked my thinking and started me along this path. Perhaps, it will do the same for you or at least give you an idea of just where it is I'm coming from. All too often, I think people leave out the thread that brought them to their conclusion or revelation; and without that beginning, I believe it leaves a gap in the logic process. One is always left with the thought of "Where did he come up with that?"

That's why I feel that this is not only an important connection but also a necessary one. You need to follow the same paths, ask the same questions, and find the same answers that I did. If you follow the same line of logic, you'll find that it was probably the same questions you once had. Besides that, it frustrates me when a teacher is teaching something, and they can't tell you the origin of the lesson or why it's done that way. At that point, they are no longer teaching, but reciting; a true teacher must know the root.

My Beginning

The root of this entire concept came to me one day while I was reading in the Book of Acts; it was where Philip was told by an angel to join an Ethiopian eunuch in his chariot. When he did, he found the Ethiopian reading from Isaiah 53. Phillip then asked the eunuch, "Do you understand what you're reading?" The eunuch replied, "How can I unless someone teaches me? Then Philip opened his mouth, and beginning at this Scripture, preached Jesus to him" (Acts 8:30–35).

Now, this was the part that began my ponderings: As they traveled on their way, the eunuch asked Philip, "See, here is water; what does stop me from being baptized?" That was a good question, I thought, but an even better one was how did he get a revelation of baptism from the Old Testament? I thought it was only a New Testament experience. I certainly didn't remember anyone getting baptized in the Old Testament, and there was no New Testament at this time; it was being formed as events like this one were unfolding. So what did this eunuch see? What did Phillip teach him that caused him to say that? For the first time in my Christian walk, I began to really think on something.

As I pondered this question over the next few weeks and months, another one came that would push my thinking a little further. This one was in the Book of John, when the Jews sent priests and Levites from Jerusalem to ask John the Baptist who he was and why was he baptizing. That seemed like a fair-enough question, especially for someone who was apparently working outside the normal parameters of the Law by baptizing in the Jordan instead of at the temple. But it was the questions they asked him that puzzled me: "Are you the Christ? . . . No, Are you Elijah? . . . No, Are you that prophet? . . . No, who then? That we may give an answer to them that sent us" (John 1:19–28).

Those were all good questions, but it was the first question that drew my attention. What was it about John's baptism that prompted them to think that he was the Christ? Now, some have said that what was really going on here was a power struggle because the Jews saw John as a threat to the temple because of his actions, but that's not true; he was just one man. What threat did he pose? And note, they asked him in the classic Jewish descending fashion: first the Christ, the most important prophetic figure to come; next was Elijah; and then that prophet, the one who would come to prepare the way for the Christ, which he was.

No, the Jews genuinely wanted to know if he was the Christ. They would have never asked him that if there was a power struggle happening. They would have threatened him at the very least and gone their way, but there was something they saw in those Old Testament scriptures that brought them out to question John, "Are you the Christ? No? Then why are you baptizing?" They saw what the eunuch would later on see. Now, the gears were really turning. What was it about baptism that brought about all these questions?

Then, the third and final thread came one night in service when the scripture was read out of 1 Peter. It was where he was speaking of how Christ suffered once for sins, the just for the unjust, that He might bring us to God and how He went and preached to all those souls before the flood. The moment of awakening came when the verse was read, "While the ark was a preparing, wherein few, that is, eight souls were saved by water. **The like figure** whereunto even baptism does now also save us" (1 Peter 3:20–21).

That phrase "the like figure" stuck out in my mind; what like figure? So what you're telling me, Peter, is that the flood was a type of baptism and a shadow of things to come, but how? And if that is the case, then there must be more of these examples in the Old Testament. The thought of it all floored me; I never knew that things such as the flood could represent aspects of the Christ and Calvary. Maybe that's what Philip showed the Ethiopian eunuch and why the priests came to question John. Could it be? And if so, surely there must be more. And there were more, more than I could have ever imagined.

When I went back to look armed with this knowledge, it was as if God opened my eyes and showed me so much more than this pattern of baptism I was following; He showed me the pattern of Calvary. All the threads in my mind were being pulled now, and the pattern that they wove was more beautiful and complex than I ever could have thought. It's been nearly eleven years now, and I'm still finding more. What's so amazing about it all is that it all started in the mind of God before He ever spoke a word of creation; it all happened like this.

> What in me is dark, illumine; what is low, raise
> and support; that to the height of this great argu-
> ment I may assert eternal providence, and justify
> the ways of God to men. (Paradise Lost)

CHAPTER 1

The Genesis

1.618

> Did I request thee, Maker, form my clay, to mold
> me man, did I solicit there from darkness to pro-
> mote me? (Paradise Lost)

Adam didn't ask to be made no more than you or I, and he certainly didn't ask to be brought into the complications and the pain of life. Nor did he ask to be judged and cast out of the only world he knew for a mistake. No, Adam just became. One day, he was nothing; and then the next, he was. Adam found himself an unwilling, subject brought into this world by a higher power that would one day seemingly abandon him over that one mistake. And perhaps, for a time, Adam believed he was special, being the only man on the earth. But in reality, he was just the first one out of the mold of what would be billions eventually created in the image of that higher power. And I assure you, he certainly did not ask to be pitted against a fallen angel known as Lucifer. Surely, God knew what the end result of that encounter would be like.

When I think about Adam's fall and the circumstances that surrounded that situation in the garden, it always bothers me. It even makes me a bit angry. How was it fair that Adam should be judged for what he did? I know he was told not to eat of that tree, but it was not entirely his fault that he faltered. As they say, "It takes two to tango." Seeing that it certainly wasn't Adam's idea to come into the world in the first place, shouldn't God then take part of the blame for creating Adam in such a way that would allow him to fail? Knowing that someone like Lucifer was on the loose, one would almost think that he was set up to fail. That's like letting your children play in the backyard, knowing there's a rattlesnake out there.

In my mind's eye, I can't help but see the whole encounter like the billing for some Las Vegas prize fight, where the announcer is standing in the middle of the ring calling out the names of the contenders and their qualities: "In this corner, wearing nothing at all, Adam and Eve," so childlike in their innocence that even the Bible said that they were naked and they knew it not. And "in the opposite corner, wearing the red trunks, Lucifer, son of the morning and the Bringer of light, the father of all lies and the fallen angel of Heavennnn!"

What's even more frustrating is that you hear people bashing Adam and Eve for their fall, like they had a choice in the whole matter. Remember that Christ was slain before the foundation of the world. Furthermore, we need to keep in mind that this was the angel that was made above all the angels, the very angel that God had fashioned perfectly: "You were perfect in your ways from the day you were created, till iniquity was found in you" (Ezekiel 28). Besides that minor detail of perfection, God only knows how old Lucifer really was at the time he deceived a third of all the angels in heaven and made open war with God. How long did he have to perfect the art of deception? It appears that his credentials in that arena are unmatched. If someone could pull that off in heaven, they can do it anywhere.

So Adam and Eve would be no contest for him. I can almost hear The Rolling Stones *Sympathy for the Devil* playing in the background as he approaches Eve for the first time in the garden:

> Please allow me to introduce myself,
> I'm a man of wealth and taste,
> I've been around for a long, long year,
> Stole many a man's soul to waste.

The odds of Adam and Eve surviving this encounter would be above a million to one; and in the spiritual realm, it must have looked like a lion stalking a toddler. Keep in mind, though, it was that deceptive ability that got Lucifer cast into the earth as punishment in the first place. This just so happened to be right in the middle of God's grandest of all undertakings, the creation of mankind. I suppose, though, after suffering such a stinging defeat, Lucifer probably figured that the best way to repay the one who just quashed all his hopes and dreams of ruling paradise was to destroy His offspring.

But instead of killing them outright, he thought it best to pervert them and turn them against their Creator, creating a sting that would last an eternity. He would repay God by destroying His hopes for children that loved Him out of choice, rather than obedience. Why kill the children of your enemy when you can poison their minds and turn them against their parents? Lucifer knew that God would not overlook disobedience, even that of these favored children; he well understood that his adversary was a god of laws and not a god of fairness. He also knew that God would punish them for their offense by casting them out of their paradise. If he lost his, then they were going to lose theirs, thus beginning the battle for everyone's return back to paradise, his and ours. I suppose Milton was right about Lucifer when he wrote, "Better to rule in hell, than to serve in heaven." Spitefulness is the destroyer of worlds.

Regardless, I really don't see how you could view this matchup any other way than an unfair fight. Lucifer deceiving Adam and Eve would be like taking candy from a baby. There was no match; it would be over in the first round. That's why it is so hard for me to understand why God dealt so harshly with them. It truly does seem like God abandoned them in their moment of need; and then, when they failed, He cast them out into the harshness of an unforgiving world. But that was on the surface; and as you'll soon learn, God never does anything on the surface.

In reality, God would never abandon the cause of man. Adam and Eve and all of mankind were just caught between the hammer and the anvil, caught between this epic struggle of good and evil. This was just all a part of God's plan to destroy the rebellion of Lucifer's once and for all. Mind you, the rebellion was not as much of a physical nature, as it was the nature of an ideal, a concept. Physical rebellions are somewhat easy to deal with. Kill enough of them, and it goes away. As the Roman historian Publius Tacitus said, "To ravage, to slaughter, to usurp under false titles, they call empire; and where they make a desert (where they kill them all), they call it peace." But the rebellions of the mind that spawn ideas against the establishment are of the most difficult nature to eradicate because they can be hidden away. So God was left with the difficult task of how to destroy the seeds of such a rebellion to prevent any further corruption of His new creation.

Moreover, Lucifer and those angels had to be dealt with in such a way that the integrity of the righteous judge of all the earth could, in fact, remain righteous. And yes, I'm sure you're thinking, couldn't God just have destroyed them right away, end of story? Sure, He could have; but remember that He created these fallen angels, meaning they were also His children. God didn't destroy them right away because I think He had a certain amount of compassion for his creation, much in the way Frankenstein had for the Monster.

Besides that, He is also a god of laws and rule; and in those laws, as Jean Valjean had said, "There is always room for mercy." No, God did not want to destroy this rebellion with force; force would not remove the idea. He would have to destroy it with a greater idea, a loftier concept; He would destroy the rebellion with the compassion of Calvary. Why else would Jesus be the "lamb slain from the foundation of the world"?

All of this brings me to my next statement, the one that has often tumbled through my thoughts. Is it really fair that we were born into this world? We didn't choose this life any more than Adam did. Yet through some strange twist of fate, here we are. Was it fair that Adam was brought here just to be pitted against Lucifer, to undo a rebellion? No. How then is it fair that we are pitted against the same creature? And please tell me, how is it fair that we are put here to develop these wonderful ties of love and compassion toward each other only to turn around one day and see one of the three Norns of Nordic fate cut the cords of those we love before our very eyes? How is it fair that we should suffer the indignity of pain and loss because someone disobeyed so long ago?

In reality, we were set up to fail this colossal test for the soul, and what seems even more unfair about the whole thing to me is that we have to choose a god, that is, if you are so inclined to be among the believing sort. Among all those faiths, there is a multiplicity of gods to choose from, with each one saying that they are the only way to Nirvana or to Heaven or to Enlightenment or to wherever the path of your choosing may lead you.

So being confronted with such a choice, how is one to be sure they have the right god or the right path? How are we to be sure that there is even a god, as no one has ever really seen Him, at least in modern times? But if there is no God, then our darkest fears would be upon us—that the evolutionists are right and that this is just a cosmic accident. If this life is all we have, then what's the use?

But let's run with that for a moment. What if we are just some cosmic accident, the one fluke in the entire universe? Can we disprove that? Sure. Did you know that it takes more faith to believe in that than it does to believe in God? I once heard that for the Big Bang to have actually happened, it would be in the realm of statistics of a 1 followed by 51 pages of typewritten zeroes behind it. Now, that's faith!

Where we can actually prove that Jesus was really here? Who was continually attesting to the validity of a god? In fact, the historian Will Durant said in his book *The Story of Civilization, Vol III: Caesar and Christ*.

> That no one reading these scenes can doubt the reality of the figure (Christ) behind them. That a few simple men should in one generation have invented so powerful and appealing a personality, so loft an ethic and so inspiring a vision of human brotherhood, would be a miracle far more incredible than any recorded in the Gospel.

So the odds are in our favor, but then, we are back to that age-old question of who is right.

So how do we determine that? How do you figure out which god is right and which is wrong? Well, it starts with some logical deduction. We already know that it is not fair that we are here, right? And no, it's not fair that we have to choose a god to serve, especially seeing that, if you get it wrong, you could spend an eternity in what most call hell. How in the world is that fair?

But by applying that same process of truthful questions to the Bible, we can logically deduce some of our answers, proving whether it is right or wrong. For example, we know our situation is not fair, but we do believe in God. So then we turn to the scripture for our answers, and we find that the Apostle Paul has already addressed this very problem of fairness in his letter to the Romans, when he wrote:

> For the Scripture says to the Pharaoh, "For this very purpose I have raised you up, that I may show my power in you (or destroy you), and that my name may be declared in all the earth." Therefore He has mercy on whom He wills, and whom He wills He hardens. You will say to me then, "**Why does He still find fault**? For who has resisted His will?" But indeed, O man, **who are you to reply against God**? Will the thing formed say to him who formed it, "Why have you made me like this?"

It's nice to know that you are not the only one who has felt this way, right? So was it fair that God hardened the heart of the pharaoh to display His power upon him? No, it was not, but who are we to complain to the one who created us? So knowing that, we can deduce that we are all stuck here, whether we like it or not. We are all caught in this quagmire of choice, literally hung between heaven and hell, where the soul's needs are pitted against our human logic.

So let me be the first to say that no, it is not fair that we have to choose the right path when so many lay before us. How in the world are we to decide the right one? I'll answer that for you—through sheer data, through the compiling of so much information that it removes all doubt of the path that you should choose, couple that with a little deductive reasoning and there you go. Now, if you don't know what deductive reasoning is, it is the process of reasoning from one or more statements or (premises) to reach a logically certain conclusion. Deductive reasoning links statements, such as verses of scriptures, with our conclusions. If all statements or premises are true, then the terms are clear, and the rules of deductive logic are followed; then, the conclusions we reach are necessarily true.

So we will approach the analysis of Calvary much in the same way we would approach a logic problem, working the formula of Calvary against the Bible until we have our conclusions. In other words, if we ask the right questions and use the pattern as our formula, then we should find the answers. It is as Savas Dimopoulos once said, "If you formulate a question properly, mathematics gives you the answer; it will carry you all the way to the truth, to the final answer." That's all we're doing here, formulating our questions in such a way that the Bible, like mathematics, will give us the final answer, leading us all the way to the truth. And so in that formulation, it is my hope that I might persuade you in going beyond believing that there is a God and into the realms of knowing that there is. Then, you will know why I choose this path and this god above all others.

Rebellion

So to start the process of this journey, and to understand some of the whys of how we got to this point, we must first go back to the beginning and actually even before that. In reality, it really all began at that rebellion, before God had ever said, "Let there be light." That was the breaking point that caused God to move forward with the project of man. He felt it was time to do something new, to create once again something divine, yet altogether different than any other thing He had done before, as John Milton had written, "Whom God's choice regard should favor equal to the sons of heaven." It was time to fulfill that prophecy that lingered in the air of heaven for so long and time to create the ones that would be just like the angels, yet a little lower in stature. It was time to create man, who was born of a desire for something more, something beyond the mechanical in thought and action, something beyond the one-time rebellious.

Now, I ask you, is it so far-fetched of an idea to think that God knew when He started to bring the earth and the cause of man to life that He would one day have to sacrifice His only Son to save this new creation? But He did. He wouldn't be God if He didn't, right? Our quote from Revelation again proves this, "Jesus Christ was the lamb slain from the foundation of the world" (Revelation 13:8). It's a concept that is often difficult for us to grasp: In the mind of God, Christ was on the cross before He ever spoke a word. But, in truth, He created everything with that in mind, even down to the placement of the planets. Despite this, I still like to believe that God's original intent for us was born of that first dream, of something pure and beautiful, something created to love and worship Him out of an obedience born of free will. And yet after our deception, instead of drawing closer to Him like rebuked little children, we have somehow all recklessly drifted far afield of that original dream.

But in retrospect, that verse of scripture assures us that He knew we would go astray because of that former rebellion. It would be the very thing that would sow the seeds of sin in our world and bring us to the point we are at today. Knowing that, it is not hard to see that the odds were against us; by that verse of scripture alone, it proves that we were destined to go astray, especially with one like Lucifer set against us. Yet destroying our paradise wasn't going to be enough for him. As time marched on, he slowly gained access to the most intimate place man had with God: the church. And why not, as Sun Tzu said, "Keep your friends close, and your enemies closer." Why the church? To twist the faith in such a way that none of us would ever find our way back. That's why there are over thirty thousand versions of Christianity today: deception. And to think, it started out with just one version a mere two thousand years ago. If left unchecked, there is no telling where we will end up.

Religion is a mere shadow of what it once was just a few decades ago. And now it seems that, in their current level of deception, men have become spellbound with size and power, completely departing from the original founder's intent and bent more on motives of greed and gain. Somewhere along the path, religion stopped being about the souls of men and more about the pocketbook. This has sadly turned religion, at least in the eyes of the people, into something like one of those B-rated sci-fi movies. You know the one where the monster escapes the lab and goes on a reign of terror; the only difference here is that it has taken us with it, dragging us along like helpless victims. But I suppose it's not entirely their fault that they have been deceived; after all, a third of the angels were also. Revenge truly is a dish best served cold, and he has it every day.

Perhaps, this was God's intent all along: to let the sick project out of the lab to infect the entire world, to cull out the weak from the strong, waiting to see which ones would survive the infection. Maybe this is, as Herbert Spencer said, "survival of the fittest," only in a spiritual sense. Because it sure seems that this disease of rebellion has been efficient in sickening our minds and propelling us in directions of faith that we were never meant to go, all in hopes of finding Him and filling that void. It's easy to see that rebellion is the root cause; what's not easy to see is our way out of this downward spiral of faith.

For religion to be where it is today, it surely means we lost something somewhere back there in the sands of time, as we are all out of place with our Creator and we know it. He righted the path once for us through Christ; but now, some two thousand years later, we find ourselves yet again off course. We want back into our paradise; but somewhere along the way, we lost the one thing that could get us back, the one thing that could cure us from the sickness that drove us out in the first place. Somewhere, we lost Calvary.

And because of that, we have become that "virus of the planet," that agent Smith called us, unable to achieve equilibrium within ourselves and our environment. Without it, we are incurable. Calvary is God's original vaccine, the cure to the disease of rebellion; and without it, man is destined for destruction. And so it is from the perspective of that unfair expulsion, that removal from Eden, that we now approach our problem, of finding our way back into Eden.

Adam

Now, I don't know if Adam ever really understood it all. But what I do know is what is written. I can tell you that, in that beginning, when God first created Adam, He loved Adam. They were friends, and for the first time, God was in love with something more than the angels. When God came down in the cool of the day to talk with Adam, it wasn't because it was a convenient time for God, but it was a time that was pleasing for Adam because the heat of the day was gone. And as time passed in their relationship, God saw that Adam was also lonely, just like Himself.

So God said, "It's not good that the man should be alone; I will make him a help mate for him" (Genesis 2:18). And as the story goes, "God caused a deep sleep to fall upon Adam, and while he slept: God took one of his ribs, and he closed up the flesh. And the rib which the Lord God had taken from man and made he a woman, and brought her unto Adam" (Genesis 2:21–24).

Through this act, God was giving Adam the relationship of a bride—the relationship He had envisioned for Himself for so long. This was not a sexual relationship, but an up close and personal relationship, the kind of closeness that only a family or two lifelong friends can share in. He knew exactly what to give Adam because it was what His idea of a relationship was to be. Moreover, by this seemingly simple act of God opening up the side of Adam and removing one of his ribs to create Eve, He was in fact foreshadowing the first of many events in the future that would take place at Calvary. At that moment, I believe God looked down through the fabric of time and saw that one day, He would finally have a bride for Himself, purchased through the side of His Christ at Calvary when the spear pierced it.

Then the soldiers came and broke the legs of the first and of the other who was crucified with Him. But when they came to Jesus and saw that He was already dead, they did not break His legs. But one of the soldiers with a spear **pierced his**

side, and forthwith came there out blood and
water. (John 19:32–34)

So you see, Adam's side was merely a foreshadow of events to
come. Not only did God see the events of Calvary in His mind's eye
long before that day ever came, but also He directed them. Just as
God had placed Adam in that deep sleep to remove his rib and give
him his bride, so too would God place His Christ in the deep sleep of
death to open His side and begin the process of receiving His bride,
which was to be the church. God guided the spear of that Roman
soldier into the side of the Christ like a surgeon's scalpel, opening it
up to allow a very symbolic blood and water to flow out.

Now, I'm sure you're thinking, why blood and water? What was
so important about that? Well, for one, it proved that He was actually dead via a process known as hypovolemic shock. The other was
that it symbolized the way in which God's new bride would come
to Him, by the blood, which symbolized His death, and by water,
which would symbolize His burial, as John said, "This is He who
came by water and blood—Jesus Christ; not only by water, but by
water and blood" (1 John 5:6).

You see, the Christ began His ministry with His baptism by
John the Baptist in the Jordan, hence the water, and finished it with
His crucifixion at Calvary, hence the blood: "not only by water, but
by water and blood." You see, what He performed in the physical, the
church would one day do in the spiritual. And these two elements are
the primary drivers for the entire book, and so as you can imagine,
we will explore them much further.

Now, I realize that this seems like a lot to go through for a
god that was lonely, but you must understand that the angels were
created to serve Him and respect Him, not to love Him. And so, in
the absence of that love, God realized the desire to create children in
His image that would not only believe in Him but also love Him by
choice. Love by choice places a certain level of devotion in one that
is not easily betrayed.

I know the idea of God subjecting Himself to the punishment
of Calvary just for a bride seems a bit crazy to us because there's never

been a god that has suffered for His followers in such a brutal way; it is usually the other way around. But what may seem crazy to us and our limited minds is and was perfectly rational to God. As Mark Twain once wrote, "Truth is stranger than fiction, but it is because Fiction is obliged to stick to possibilities; Truth isn't."

But, as usual with God, there was a deeper meaning being transmitted here, and that was the love a man ought to have for his bride. God was displaying the kind of love that will oftentimes push a man beyond the point of his own will and into dire situations. This was the kind of love that was needed to send His only Son to the cross, as John wrote, "For God so loved the world, that He gave His only begotten son" (John 3:16). And it is that same desire that God has fashioned into us, so that we could identify with His desire and willingness to go the distance for something He loved.

The Apostle Paul confirms the concept of loving something so much that one is willing to die for it when he wrote to the Ephesians, "Therefore be imitators of God as dear children. And walk in love, as Christ also has loved us and **given Himself** for us, an offering and a sacrifice to God for a sweet-smelling aroma" (Ephesians 5:1–2).

He went on to say that husbands should love their wives to the extent that they should be willing to die for them as Christ died for the church, finalizing the concept for us when he said:

> So husbands ought to love their own wives as their own bodies; he who loves his wife loves himself. For no one ever hated his own flesh, but nourishes and cherishes it, just as the Lord does the church. For we are members of His body, of His flesh and of His bones. For this reason a man shall leave his father and mother and be joined to his wife, and **the two shall become one flesh. This is a great mystery, but I speak concerning Christ and the church.** (Ephesians 5:28–32)

You must understand that the story of Adam and Eve was nothing more than a well-orchestrated allegory of Christ and the church.

Just as Adam became one with Eve, so one day we will die and become one with Christ. That's what it is all about—moving from that transitory, fleeting physical state that we are in now to that spiritual eternal state of oneness with our savior someday. So, through the first man Adam, a physical bride was created; and through this second man, the Christ, a spiritual bride was created. This also extends to us and our relationship with God. We first become the physical bride through conversion and then become the spiritual bride in death.

The Fall

So, after God had created Eve from Adam's side, all things seem to be going well. The statement was even made by Adam declaring their unity: "This is now bone of my bone and flesh of my flesh: she shall be called woman, because she was taken out of man" (Genesis 2:23–25). Though the Bible is somewhat vague on the life of Adam and Eve, there is enough history written in these few pages that we can paint a picture of their lives and their condition and come to some solid conclusions.

In just a few verses, we read, "And they were both naked, the man and his wife, and they were not ashamed." They were innocent to begin with, the harmless children of God living in paradise. But in just a few more verses, we find something evil has entered into the garden paradise in the form of a fallen angel and is preparing to make spoil of these innocent children. By the time this angel is done with them and the deception is complete, their eyes will be well opened to the knowledge of good and evil:

> Now the serpent was more cunning than any
> beast of the field which the Lord God had made.
> And he said to the woman, "Has God indeed
> said, 'you shall not eat of every tree of the gar-
> den'?" And the woman said to the serpent, "We
> may eat the fruit of the trees of the garden; but
> of the fruit of the tree which is in the midst of
> the garden, God has said, 'You shall not eat it,

nor shall you touch it, lest you die.'" Then the
serpent said to the woman, "You will not surely
die. For God knows that in the day you eat of
it your eyes will be opened and you will be like
God, knowing good and evil." (Genesis 3:1–4)

In every good lie or deception, there is an element of truth in it.
The serpent didn't lie when he told her that she should know good
and evil, for she surely did when she ate off the fruit; the lie was
about the death. God never meant that it was to be an instant death,
like when one eats something poisonous, but that they would lose
the ability to live forever, being banished from the garden and the
tree of life. So began the fall from paradise:

And the eyes of them both were open, and they
knew that they were naked; and they sewed fig
leaves together and made themselves aprons. And
they heard the voice of the Lord God walking in
the garden in the cool of the day: and Adam and
his wife hid themselves from the presence of the
Lord God among the trees of the garden. And the
Lord God called unto Adam, and said unto him,
where are you? And he said, I heard your voice in
the garden, and I was afraid, because I was naked;
and I hid myself. And he said, who told you that
you were naked? (Genesis 3:7–11)

So the deed was done and the fall now well in progress; all things
were going according to plan, as Lucifer had most certainly sworn to
destroy God's new creation. But it wasn't in the manner that most
of us would have thought. Why not kill them? No, he wanted to do
something more malicious than killing them. He wanted to corrupt
them and infect them with the cancerous seeds of rebellion. What
better way to repay your foe than to turn His children against Him?
Lucifer knew that perverting His enemy's children would be
far worse than killing them because he knew the righteousness of

THE PATTERN OF CALVARY

God would reject them just as he was rejected, but what he could not foresee was God's willingness to go the distance for His children. How could he? He was blinded by his hatred and bitterness for them; he hated the fact that God loved them and gave them a paradise that he felt entitled to, and the fact that these inferior beings now had a greater position in the earth than him further fueled the rage. Who were they compared to him? He was the flower of heaven, not them; they were merely the flowers of earth. No, to kill them would be too good for them; they must suffer as he was suffering. He knew that the sooner the innocence was gone, the sooner they could start their own personal rebellion and fall from that heavenly position just as he did. And though the paradise of heaven and earth were in some disorder, with children falling from grace on either end, all was not hopeless. God had already foreseen all of this and devised a plan to redeem His creation. That plan or blueprint is what we are about to examine. As you will see, it redeemed His people back then, and it will redeem us today.

So the first part of God's grand design was quite obvious. God wanted His relationship with man back; He wanted His bride that had been stolen by sin. Second, He would have to have a way to redeem His bride, a way of purifying her. Third, He needed someone to lead the bride, to help point the way until the time of redemption. What you are about to learn is what modern religion has lost or buried from us, but the winds of change have now blown long enough to move aside the sands of deceit to reveal what has been lost to us for so long. This is our way back to God; we know what the matrix is now—religion—and we know how we got here, but the journey out is not so easily summed up. This begins your journey out, Alice.

> You see, there is only one constant, one univer-
> sal truth, causality, action and reaction, cause
> and effect. Choice is an illusion, created between
> those with power and those without, this is the
> nature of the universe, we struggle against it, we
> fight to deny it, but it is of course a lie, the truth
> is, we are completely out of control. Causality,

there is no escape from it, we are forever slaves to it, our only hope is to understand it, to understand the why. Why is what separates us from them, you from me. Why is the only real power, without it you are powerless. It is the question that drives us. (*The Matrix*)

CHAPTER 2

The Sacrifice

Blood Red

> And how can man die better than facing fearful
> odds, for the ashes of his fathers, and the temples
> of his Gods? (Thomas Babington Macaulay)

After Adam and Eve had eaten that cursed fruit and fallen from
grace, God came down for His evening visit and found them hiding
in the garden. Now that their eyes were opened, they were trying to
cover their nakedness—and their mistake—as children usually do,
but not with lies, with fig leaves; unfortunately, those fig leaves were
an inadequate covering for their sins. It seems that our concepts for
covering sin are never what God's are. There is nothing man can do
to hide his sins from God, and only God can devise a plan sufficient
enough to rid man of his sins. So, because of this sin, God placed a
curse on them both:

> To the woman He said: "I will greatly multiply
> your sorrow and your conception; in pain you
> shall bring forth children; your desire shall be for
> your husband, and he shall rule over you." Then
> to Adam He said, "Because you have heeded the
> voice of your wife, and have eaten from the tree

of which I commanded you, saying, 'You shall not eat of it': "Cursed is the ground for your sake; in toil you shall eat of it all the days of your life. Both thorns and thistles it shall bring forth for you, and you shall eat the herb of the field. In the sweat of your face you shall eat bread till you return to the ground, for out of it you were taken; for dust you are, And to dust you shall return." (Genesis 3:16–19)

And before He drove them out of the garden and placed that angel at the entrance to guard it, God did what must have seemed unusual and quite frightening to both Adam and his bride: "And unto Adam also and to his wife did the Lord God make coats of skins, and clothed them." (Genesis 3:20–21)

Now, let's not be naive here; the only way to get the skins of these animals, and to cover the naked sin of both Adam and Eve, was to kill these animals or sacrifice them. Up until this point, the garden had been a paradise: There was no death and certainly no bloodshed. But all of that changed after that one mistake. Death had now entered into the world. These were not only the first deaths recorded in the Bible but also the first of many sacrifices in a plan to redeem mankind.

You see, by the sacrificing of these animals, God would set a type, or a standard, that would become a Biblical institution forever: The shedding of innocent blood was necessary to cover the sins of the guilty. And for the time being, the blood of the sacrifices would hold at bay the wrath of God until the time of reformation, when that perfect blood could be shed to satisfy the judgments of God. So, from that moment until Moses and the law, it would be set in the stone of tradition that the Christ would come and shed His blood to remove this curse once and for all, as the Lord yet gave a glimmer of this hope in the dealing out of the curses, as He told the serpent, "And I will put enmity between you and the woman, and between your seed and her Seed; He shall bruise your **head**, and you shall bruise His **heel**" (Genesis 3:15).

In the foreshadowing of that prophesy, God was alluding to the day that the bringer of death, the serpent, would have his head crushed by the very one he would try to destroy, the Christ. God was saying that even though you will bring death to Him on that day, it shall be but a small thing, as if biting His heel, but His death will be a fatal blow to your head—It will be the destruction of the fear that you brought to mankind. His death will undo what you have done this day in the garden; His death will undo death itself. So, if by one man death came to us all, so it must be in the order of things: Another man's death brings forth life. "For as by one man's disobedience many were made sinners, so also by one Man's obedience many will be made righteous" (Romans 5:19).

I wonder sometimes if God ever explained to Adam and Eve why He had to kill the animals to cover their now-naked bodies or if they were just left in the dark, left in their sin and guilt like so many of us, wondering why something innocent had to die because of them. I wonder how they must have felt being driven from that garden paradise that day into the harsh environment of an unknown and untamed world. Utterly alone and helpless, I suppose. It seems to be the path so many of us go down.

Blood

Now, for those of us with just a basic understanding of the Bible, this act of killing these animals served a twofold purpose; not only did the animal give its life, but also there had to be bloodshed. Just killing the animal without bloodshed would not be enough. But then that leaves us with some questions. What purpose did the blood serve, and why wasn't the life enough? Concerning the blood, it is as God said in Leviticus17:11: "For the life of the flesh is in the blood." You see, blood sustains life. Because there is an individual life in the blood, no blood no life, but let me explain.

You see blood is, in and of itself, a very complex organism that works together with its platelets and white cells to sustain life. Depleting this vital life-giving system from any organism means sure death. Blood and life are intermingled; they are one and the same, and yet, there is a deeper connection with the blood here, and that's concerning its water content. We all know that nothing can survive without water, and water is also at the very core of blood's sustaining power. Plasma, which is the liquid portion of the blood, is almost 92% water. There is an unbreakable connection that exists between these two elements. Interestingly enough, it was both blood and water that flowed from the side of Christ, but this connection is too expansive for one chapter. We will explore that later on. As for now, the blood's primary biblical purpose was, first, to replicate the shed blood of Christ at Calvary and, second, to pay the debt of sin; it is the only thing that God will accept as payment. So, along with the taking of a life, the blood works together to redeem a life from hell; you see, the blood pays the debt, and the life force redeems. They work together in a spiritual platform much in the same way as blood works with its platelets and white blood cells, only they are working together to secure one's soul.

But again, we are back to why. Why this way? For that answer, we need to go back to the beginning again; remember that Christ is the "lamb slain from the foundation of the world." Before God ever said, "Let there be light," in His mind, not only did He see the brutal slaying of the Christ, but also He designed it that way. He designed it so that the Christ would shed His blood and die on that cross because He chose blood to be the only thing that can hold back the sin of death that had recently entered the world. I know it is a coun-terintuitive process to require death in lieu of the death of a soul, but it is a soul we are talking about here after all. And these sacrifices were just the shadows of that future death of the Christ.

You see, those first deaths were just a part of God's grand design, one that He had established from the beginning, a design that would be built with blood. So the process literally becomes a blood in, blood out process; sin created in us the need for blood to cover that sin in the eyes of God, and the precious blood of Christ is the very thing that will take us out of here and into heaven. Unfortunately, there is no other way to get there; our sins in the eyes of God are just too vulgar.

But I suppose that poses the much larger question: Why did He design it that way? Why did He choose to send His only Son to die for us in such a way? That I cannot say for sure. I know if I were God, I would have chosen something much less violent; but then again, "His thoughts and His ways are far above ours" (Isaiah 55:9). Undoubtedly, He was angling for our heartstrings. What I do know is that He would give His only Son, and He would model everything after that feature. And for whatever the reason was, He chose blood as the currency to pay the debt of sin and hold back His judgments until that perfect sinless blood of the Christ could be shed.

Cain and Abel

So, as time moved on, we see this foundation of sacrifice and bloodshed being adopted by them and their offspring, Cain and Abel. Like so many of us, they must not have known why the shedding of blood was so important and what it represented, as they both brought two very different sacrifices before God.

> And in the process of time it came to pass, that Cain brought his sacrifice of the fruit of the land, a ground offering unto the Lord. And Abel, he also brought his sacrifice of the firstlings of his flock and of the fat thereof. And the Lord had respect unto Abel and to his offering. But unto Cain and his offering he had no respect. And Cain was very angry and his countenance fell. (Genesis 4:3–5)

Why did God have respect for Abel's sacrifice and not Cain's? This was because Abel's fit the pattern God had already set with his parents as a foreshadowing of redemption, and the sacrificing of the finest of the flocks was a part of it. Again, in hindsight, we see this as the Christ who was ordained from the beginning to suffer death and to shed His innocent blood to cover once and for all the sins of the guilty and to break this curse of death. But what we haven't seen so clearly about this whole process of sacrifice is how it relates to us and our Christian walk. Sure, we can see how the animals and Christ are linked: through the innocence and the blood. As John the Baptist said, "Behold the Lamb of God which takes away the sins of the world." There's nothing that invokes the image of innocence quite like a lamb, is there?

Sacrifice

But for all of that and those limited connections, we have never really understood how Christ's death and our sins were to be so intertwined. If you ask me, some of the first questions anyone should ask if they are seriously considering becoming a Christian are as follows: "What connects me to all of this?" "Why is all of this Old Testament stuff important?" It's important to us because not only were these sacrifices a foreshadow of the death of Christ, but also they were showing us the principle on which sacrifice is built on. Sacrifice, at least in the biblical context, goes far beyond the concept of just offering objects to a higher power. It is the giving of something valuable to a God, or a cause, that is far greater than oneself, and that is the example that has always been set before us in the scriptures.

So in Abel's case, he was sacrificing the finest and first of his flocks because the Christ was to be the finest and the first of God's flock. Moreover, because of the level of quality that God would send for that sacrifice, it surely meant that fulfilling the mere shadow of it was going to cost something as well. Just look at what it nearly cost Abraham when he was told to sacrifice Isaac. Yet in return for fulfilling the type as prescribed, God would count it as righteousness, meaning one's actions are justified and pleasing to God.

So you see, sacrifice gave all those that were before Calvary the ability to stay the judgments of God simply because God designed those animals to be a shadow of the Christ. As the writer of Hebrews said:

> For **if** the blood of bulls and goats, and the ashes
> of an heifer sprinkling the unclean, sanctified to

> the purifying of the flesh: (if those thing made them clean, then) How much more shall the blood of Christ, who through the eternal Spirit offered himself without spot to God. (Hebrews 9:13–14)

In short, God designed the entire process to be a shared relationship of sacrifice and salvation, meaning that if He was going to sacrifice His Son to save man, then man should have to sacrifice something near and dear to save himself. And so today, the thing that allows us to partake in the symbolic death, or sacrifice of Christ, as all those former souls did through the animals, is through the act of what we call repentance. It is the sacrificing of our former lives, which oftentimes are near and dear to us, and turning to the lifestyle of Christ. Repentance in its purest form simply means to turn around, to turn from the life direction you were on and go the direction of Christ.

This new form of symbolic death exists for us today because we cannot physically go and shed our own blood and die to remove our sins. Our lives are tainted by our former sins, but Christ was not, hence the reasoning for Him to be sinless. Seeing that animal sacrifice was removed some time ago after His death, we are left with no other choice but to repent. Besides that is not what God expects from us today. Sacrificing of one's physical self would put you in the same position as Cain: It would be an offering of selfishness. No, what God wants from us is to live for Him, not to die, at least in the physical sense. Christ has taken care of that part. The death that God wants from us now is the crucifixion of our own will and rising and walking in newness of life following Him.

As Jesus himself said, "For whoever desires to save his life will lose it, but whoever **loses his life** for my sake will find it. For what profit is it to a man if he gains the whole world, and loses his own soul?" (Matthew 16:25–26).

He wasn't speaking of a physical death there, but it was a death of lifestyle, a death of things that are contrary to God, dying to your worldly lust and living for Him. And what do we receive in return for that sacrifice? God in return pays the debt of your sins with the blood of Christ, thus justifying you in His eyes.

We even find that Jesus was obedient to this symbolic principle of sacrifice to one's will and repentance. Seeing that He left us a beautiful example of it when He was in the garden praying just before His crucifixion, as He said, "O My Father, if it is possible, let this cup pass from me; **nevertheless, not as I will, but as you will**" (Matthew 26:39). He was saying, "I want to live, but I know you want me to die." Christ turned from His will to live and to the will of God and offered Himself for a sacrifice. And again, we likewise share or partake in His death today through this symbolic act of repentance. Now, I know it may not be so clear now, but as we move along it will become clearer. Just know that this is our first step back to understanding what God wants from the believer. It's always been this way, even from the beginning.

So to sum up our understanding about sacrifice and the blood, we turn to the writer of Hebrews, "And almost all things are by the law purged with blood; and without the shedding of blood is no remission" (Hebrews 9:22). Reading this verse, one might question what is placed in remission when blood is shed. Sin is, but how? This is by the taking of a life and with the shedding of innocent blood to remit the offense. You understand that the animal's blood was used because they were innocent. Animals cannot sin; therefore, their blood cannot be tainted. That's why God required their blood: It was the closest thing He had to the blood of Christ.

This is why God was so specific in the types of sacrifices He wanted to atone for sin: They had to fit the pattern of His Christ. When you see the phrase in the Bible "without spot or blemish," it means without sin—perfect; the sacrifices had to be the best a person had to offer because God would be giving His best to redeem His lost creation at Calvary. God's first type of Calvary was now set with the death of the innocent to pay for the sins of the guilty, and He set it with the scarlet blood of a sacrifice.

I often wonder just how long we were to be left in the dark concerning sacrifices. Were we to always be like Cain and Abel, ignorant of what we do and why? I think it was Einstein who said, "What does the fish know of the water it swims in?" In like response, what do we know of the God we serve? Most of us have never really had this explained. There's been such a gap in our understanding as to how all these sacrifices were shadows of the Christ to come and how it all related to us. Benito Mussolini once said about history, "Blood alone moves the wheels of history," and so it is the same for the Bible. Blood alone moves the wheels of the Bible. Rivers of blood have been spilt in the course of redeeming God's beloved.

> I hear you say "why?" Always "why?" You see things; and you say "why?" But I dream things that never were; and I say "why not?" (George Bernard Shaw)

CHAPTER 3

❧

The Womb of Creation

Blue

> Instruct me, for thou know'st: thou from the first
> wast present, and, with mighty wings outspread,
> dove-like sat'st brooding on the vast abyss and
> mad'st it pregnant. (Paradise Lost)

So after the due course of time, man's ignorance of the needs of God grew ever wider, as apparently the reasoning behind the need for those animal sacrifices was lost to all but one man, Noah. I suppose Cain never did learn the reason behind the why of sacrifice; as for Abel, well his blood and probably many others would cry out from the ground for judgment upon all humanity, which would come in the form of the flood.

Now, before we can move into the flood and its many lessons God had placed there for us, we first need to understand why this flood was coming. And for that to happen, you'll first need to see the flood as something other than a judgment. Because believe me, it would be more than just the sins of man that would bring this destruction crashing down upon the earth. Sadly though, it's been that kind of narrow-minded view of the whole event that has kept us from seeing the flood for what it truly was. And that's because we as believers have always either viewed, or been told, that that's exactly what it was—a fitting punishment for all those souls that had sinned so much against a righteous God that it forced Him to bring this destruction upon the earth and send all those wicked souls to hell.

Now, I understand that part of that rationale stems from the fact that we ourselves are very judgmental by nature. Sprinkle that with a little religious self-righteousness, and it becomes easy to see the whole thing as a judgment. As we all know, it's certainly a lot easier to justify punishment if we believe it is deserved and even easier to see others sent to hell for their disobedience, rather than see ourselves there for the same infractions. In short, all that self-righteousness has blinded us from seeing past what was truly a superficial judgment.

So in order for us to understand the real meaning behind this coming flood and how it ties into Calvary, we will have to once again go back to the beginning of creation, back to that day one and see this from God's perspective to truly understand His motives. Because you see, God did not see or design the flood to be the total destruction of man, though it was an intended side effect; but, as always with God, there was a much more profound reason behind it all. The paramount object lesson here that God was trying to transmit to us, was that this flood was going to be the rebirth of humanity and not its destruction. That apparent judgment of man was only on the surface; it was simply a judgment and destruction of the flesh of man and not the eternal soul. Why not the soul? Because there was no Law at that time to judge and convict the soul with.

I ask you, how can you judge someone when there are no rules or laws to judge them by? The simple answer is you can't. I know some have said that there were rules and laws at that time for man to follow, but they can't seem to produce the first one for me, save the institution of sacrifice. So again, how can you judge the eternal soul that the sins in the temporary flesh were committed against when there was no written Law? The actual Law was not going to come for almost another two thousand years with the arrival of Moses. So God's only recourse of punishment at that time for a sinful society was to destroy the body; the eternal soul's judgment would have to wait upon the Law. "The sting of death is sin; and the strength of sin is the law" (1 Corinthians 15:56).

Of course, this principle of judgment does not go unfounded, as we find that the Apostle Paul addressed this very concept for us in his letter to the Romans,

> Therefore, just as through one man (Adam) **sin** entered the world, and **death** through sin, and **thus death spread to all men,** (not condemnation) because all sinned. For **until the law** sin was in the world, **but sin is not imputed** (seen as fault) **when there is no law**. Nevertheless, **death** reigned (but not judgment) from Adam (the bringer of death) to Moses (the giving of the law), even over those who **had not sinned** according to the likeness of the transgression of Adam, who is a type of Him (Christ) who was to come. (Romans 5:12–14)

So you see, Adam brought sin into the world, but its only consequence was death. And believe me, that's not a minor thing, but it did not bring eternal judgment. That could not come until there was a Law established, and again, that wasn't going to happen until Moses came and led the Israelites into the wilderness. But then the question arises, what happened to all those souls?

Well, it was for that very reason that Jesus, while He was buried those three days after His crucifixion, went into what the Bible calls the "lower parts" of the earth to retrieve those souls that were before the flood and the Law and to offer them a chance at redemption, which I'm sure they gladly accepted. Now, how do I know this? The Apostle Peter confirmed this for us when he wrote:

> For Christ also suffered once for sins, the just for the unjust, that He might bring us to God, being put to death in the flesh but made alive by the Spirit, by whom also **He went and preached to the spirits in prison,** who **formerly** were disobedient, **when once the Divine longsuffering**

> **waited in the days of Noah**, while the ark was
> being prepared, in which a few, that is, eight souls,
> were saved through water. (1 Peter 3:18–20)

So I ask you, if God passed eternal judgment on all those souls as we have always believed, then who are these that Peter is writing about? Not convinced, Paul further backs up this concept when he writes to the Ephesians,

> But to each one of us grace was given accord-
> ing to the measure of Christ's gift. Therefore He
> says: "When He ascended on high, **He led cap-
> tivity captive, and gave gifts to men**." Now this,
> "He ascended"—what does it mean **but that He
> also first descended into the lower parts of the
> earth?** He who descended is also the One who
> ascended far above all the heavens, that He might
> fulfill all things. (Ephesians 4:7–10)

Again, who were these people that were led from captivity into a heavenly captivity, unless they were those that were before the flood? So you see, God could not condemn the souls of mankind until the Law came, not if He is, as Abraham called Him, "The righteous judge of all the earth." He could only allow death to take you from the physical, hence the saying that "death reigned from Adam to Moses." Death was the only legal recourse that could come upon man; it was the harshest sentence that God could pass without a Law being in place, and I only mention this in such detail because there is a greater unfolding to it all later on. "And these times of this ignorance God overlooked; but now commands all men everywhere to repent" (Acts17:30).

And since we're here, we might as well touch on the other reason why Jesus had to descend into the "lower parts of the earth." You see, He also went to take the keys of death and hell, as John wrote in the book of Revelation, "I am He (Christ) who lives, and was dead, and behold, I am alive forevermore. Amen. And I have **the keys of**

Hades and **of Death**" (Revelation 1:18). Why did He have to do that? To undo the death that Adam's sin had brought into the world and the fear that it has placed humanity in from that time until now, thus destroying that holding place that was created by sin and giving the eternal soul the ability to bypass hell. When Christ rose from the grave, He undid the very thing that humanity thought could never be undone—death.

The writer of Hebrews confirmed the destruction of the fear of death when he wrote:

> Inasmuch then as the children have partaken of flesh and blood, He Himself (Christ) likewise shared in the same, **that through death** He might **destroy him who had the power of death**, that is, **the devil**, (AKA the serpent) and **release** those who through fear of death were all their lifetime **subject to bondage**. (Hebrews 2:14–16)

When Christ took those symbolic keys and rose from the place that no man was ever supposed to rise from, He would crush death's grip on humanity and set us free from that fear forever. Remember the curse placed on the serpent back in the garden, that his head would be crushed? This was that prophesy coming to fruition. "O death, where is thy sting? O grave, where is thy victory?" (1 Corinthians 15:55).

So you see, the death of Christ did more than just remove the sins of the world. It was also done to justly redeem those who died without a Law and to remove the curse of death that was brought about by Adam's mishap in the garden. And so, just as the death of Christ had more than one purpose, the flood also carried more than one reason for coming. It was so much more than a judgment upon humanity as you'll soon see.

Now, I know the flood doesn't appear to be that way, especially with comments by God like "I'm sorry I made them," but that was on the surface. That statement is what's known as an equivocal statement, meaning that the phrase carries more than one meaning to it.

Oftentimes God's statements are in layers, meaning that there will be the literal side of it, which is true, and then there is the symbolic side, which is a little more elusive. It's not an easy task to decipher them, but it's done through deductive logic.

So, the moment that appeared to be the breaking point of God's patience was in reality only a starting date to the countdown of the destruction of man, and though it would take some 120 years from this point to bring the flood, God would soon have His next typeset. Now, before we move on in our teardown of water, I think this verse of scripture also gives us a good opportunity to further explore God's use of language. Understanding how the language of the Bible functions is a critical step in our process of interpreting its many transmitted meanings. This can be at times difficult to understand, but if we are to fully grasp the flood or any other of the Bible's symbolic messages, then we first need to understand how God uses language and metaphors to veil His true intent. Hidden behind those words you will discover His motives, and if you understand the motive, you understand the whys. As Mark Twain once said, "The two most important days in your life are the day you are born and the day you find out why."

Language

That's because the whys are not only life questions but also are the true drivers behind all the biblical construction and symbolism; knowing why God did a thing gives us the ability to look behind the coded veil of language to see the actual reasoning for all the events. And, for us, discovering the whys of the Bible unlocks something in our minds that can never easily be undone; they generate within us that "Aha moment" or "moment of revelation." This is a moment of coming to a sudden understanding of a previously incomprehensible problem or concept; it is an experience that is, as far as we know, unique to humans. As researchers have discovered, when a human comes to that sudden understanding of why a thing is done or said a certain way, it gives them a certain amount of joy and satisfaction. It also gives them the ability to process the newfound information much more fluently and accurately. Perhaps, that's why God wrote the Bible in such a way, so that we could have those "moments of revelation" to stimulate our minds and to have a greater recall of the scripture.

And interestingly enough, the entire process is done through language. As we know, God never used actual symbols in the Bible to illustrate His messages. Instead, it was all done through language, and that's probably because He understood our tendency toward the worship of such things. For example, the bronze serpent that Moses was instructed to make and raise up in the wilderness for the healing of those who had been bitten by the serpents later became a symbol of false worship to the Israelites known as Nehushtan. So because of that propensity to drift, God gave us language instead of symbols.

Language is also far superior to symbols because language can be infinitely more symbolic than the actual symbols themselves. Symbols are limited in their ability to transmit information. Why? Because all symbols have a material form to them, which means that though they can be very complex, the basic message never changes, and once you discover their meaning, the transmission of information is complete. You can get nothing more out of them. Whereas, words work by combining one or more sounds to create a specific meaning assigned by that language, and that's the major advantage to the human language being a learned symbolic communication system. It maintains that "infinite flexibility."

Because meanings can be changed and new symbols created for each word, new words are created every day to support our ever-changing language. And therein lies part of the reason why the Bible remains one of the most cryptic books in the world. Not only are you compounding words and phrases to acquire their meanings and symbolisms, but also you are trying to understand the intent behind those words to extract the motives and to get beyond that nagging question of "why did God do that?" Factoring intent in itself is not an easy task either, as God rarely gives a reason why He did something. This forces us to read between the lines to extract the true meanings. God's intentions often cannot be read on the literal surface; but, instead, they like to flee from the intrusion of man by hiding themselves in His symbolisms and allegories, only revealing their true depths to those who are diligent enough to pursue them there. If you don't think that's true, just read the Book of Ezekiel. If that's not an allegorical riddle, then please tell me what is.

Just because we think we know Him doesn't mean we understand Him, and so likewise with His speech, it cannot be nailed down to just one single meaning. It is both literal and figurative; it is telling, and yet it is veiled; it is coded, and yet it is plain; and it almost always carries a multiplicity of meanings. If you don't believe that, just take a look at Ivan Panin's work concerning the conversion of verbal scriptures to numeric values; in doing so, what he discovered was an extremely complex numbering system that saturated every book of the Bible, revealing a whole sublayer of types and shadows that were far beyond the normal. So much so that he said, "If human logic is worth anything at all, we are simply driven to the conclusion that if my facts I have presented are true, then man could never have done this." He understood that there was no way mankind could have ever put together such a complex and redundant set of patterns throughout the course of one book spanning a period of roughly 2,000 years by forty different writers from three continents, who wrote in three different languages. Man's level of intelligence was just not there, especially on a mathematical level, which was required to create patterns of this magnitude, spanning not only numbers and coded writings but also colors and veiled symbolic meanings. This was all done through the use of words.

And so it is through this complex medium of language that He chose to communicate with us. Mind you, it was not through mathematics or symbolism, because those methods are limited in their ability to transmit information. But through the use of language God could not only express His symbolic and mathematical messages but also transmit concepts and ideas, metaphors, and allegories, all without any limitations to the believer. So the use of language and wordplay is something that is very important to God. The written word of the Bible is in essence the verbal transmission of His thoughts and ideals. It is the expression of the intent of the heart: "For out of the abundance of the heart the mouth speaks" (Luke 6:45).

Understanding the simple fact that God layers His speech helps us in understanding the symbolic nature of the Bible, and once you know how to peel back the layers, you begin to understand the whys. He layers His speech just like His allegories. Keep in mind that His layered speech never contradicts itself or its designs. In fact, it supports them, and it is in perfect harmony with everything He does. Yes, the Bible's language is complex, but it's important for us to understand God's speech and how He hides His true motive behind it. They kind of go hand in hand. One's actions are usually telling of their thoughts.

I'm Sorry I Made Them

Now, this portion of scripture that we touched on earlier was just one aspect of the phrase because underneath it, when God said, "I'm sorry I made them," it wasn't really in the context, or framework, that we would normally think it was in. So by using a little logical deduction, we arrive at some really good questions like, if He was truly sorry for creating man, then why didn't He end it all right there? Why didn't He just make another Adam and have another go at it? He could have started over a thousand times if He wanted to.

So then, why did He move forward with the project of man if He was so upset with their actions? It's because His motives in that statement were ulterior—They were hidden. God didn't end it all because He wasn't sorry for the reasons we think He was sorry for. I know we like to think that God was completely disgusted with humanity at that point, but appearances aren't everything, especially when it comes to God. There always seems to be a deeper meaning lurking just beneath the surface with Him; and this is, if anything, a good lesson on how He veils His speech. Again, one's actions are telling of one's thoughts and intent.

So then returning to our question, what was He sorry about? He was sorry about His decision to go forward with this whole project—not for His sake, mind you, but for the sake of mankind. Don't get me wrong; He knew this day was coming. If He didn't know that this was the end result of humanity, then He's not God, now is He?

The thing is, though, I don't think He fully equated the emotional factor into His design. What I mean by that is how many times have we said that we were going to do something, but when it came time, we had second thoughts, and our emotions kicked in and changed our minds?

I believe at that moment, when He was about to destroy all of mankind, He took a second look down through time itself as He did with Adam's rib and saw the incredible amount of pain and suffering that was going to befall mankind over the entire course of this project of redemption. I think He viewed the cost and was truly sorry for what He was about to put not only man through but also His Son; "this is going to hurt me more than it's going to hurt you" kind of comes to mind. God was literally torn between two emotional worlds, where on one hand He would watch His creation die, falling under His judgments, yet on the other hand He would see its rebirth, brought about by His mercy. It would be a bittersweet day for God when the floods finally came, but make no mistake, setting the type overrode all emotions; He had to do what was best for humanity. So, yes, He was sorry; but it wasn't for the reasons that we think it was for.

So you see, by slowly tearing down that old belief system of the flood solely being a judgment and starting the process of introducing new concepts and information into the event, we begin to paint a fuller picture of what the flood was truly about, thus giving us a greater insight into God's actions. Because once you see that the flood and other events like it were not just the knee-jerk reactions of an all-powerful God to things as they transpired on earth, but, rather, the well-thought-out premeditated events that He had intended them to be. You then begin to realize the depth in which God has orchestrated every event of the Bible, down to the smallest of details, even going as far as inspiring the names of those people who would be used in these grand designs.

Noah

Since we are talking about the flood, let's take the name of Noah, for instance, which means "rest." So if we apply that in a metaphorical sense to our story, the interpreted outcome is, then, that through this man Noah and his rebirth into a new world via the flood, God would grant the earth rest from the sins of man. This, of course, would be a faint shadow of the resurrection of the Christ when one day, He would rise above the sins of the world like that Ark, via the tomb, and be granted rest, or Noah, from His labors in the flesh. And in doing so, He would open the door to all those who come unto Him for that same "Noah" as He said, "Come unto me, all ye that labor and are heavy laden, and I will give you rest" (Matthew11:28).

But my point to that little side road there is that God so designed the life of Noah that in form, it would mirror the actual substance of the life of Christ. So much so that, once you see it, it becomes difficult to see the story of the flood any other way than just another pattern that was used to build the image of Calvary. Comparatively, we also see the similarities between the Ark and the tomb of Christ in that they both became vessels of transition from one phase of life to the other, moving each man from certain death to life again.

Interestingly enough, we also find that both of them had the doors to those vessels moved by the hand of God. In Noah's case, God closed the door when he entered the Ark; and, in Christ's case, the door or stone was rolled away, thus opening the tomb, as if to symbolically say, "That this allegory began with Noah, and it ended with Christ." So you see, the Ark was nothing more than a symbolic tomb that Noah would one day rise from, just as the Christ would one day rise from His symbolic Ark, which was nothing more than a tomb.

Now that we have that out of the way and our views of the flood are beginning to change, we can now move on to the more complex symbolism of the flood. Because the flood is one of the main setups of the entire Bible, it is the foundation that constitutes a third of its symbolic meaning; the other two thirds are wrapped up in the death and resurrection.

So if you miss the meaning of this concept here as almost all of religion has, you'll miss a third of what Calvary and the Bible was all about. This is one of the primary reasons why modern religion is in the shape it is in today. They have misplaced the fundamental principles of the Bible. Somewhere, they missed the biblical class on how 2+2 works, and they tried to go straight to algebra. You understand that without a baseline of knowledge, you really can't move on to more complex equations, and the same holds true for the Bible. Missing the fundamentals has left our understanding of the Bible in such a state of deficiency that it has made it ineffectual in transmitting its true message, but really who is to blame? In some way, we all are, for not doing our due diligence sooner. This is just one of those subjects that we'll need to be unfolded with great care so you can absorb it fully.

The Flood

So, what was the flood besides a superficial judgment? Well, as I said before, it was to be the rebirth of humanity. So then what did we miss in this flood for that to be its primary objective? Well for starters, what we missed was the fact that everything in the Bible hinges on those three basic concepts of death, burial, and resurrection; and again, to miss just one of those foundational principles in its beginnings was enough to leave huge gaps in our overall biblical understanding. That's simply because by the sheer laws of nature, things just don't seem to make sense when you have missed the first lesson. You have to have that baseline foundation in order to expand your knowledge in any subject.

So if it's not explained to you now, you're certainly not going to get it later on, as these allegorical concepts were designed to be progressive in nature just like mathematics, building upon one another and growing slightly more complex with each addition to the pattern. God designed it so that once one lesson was complete, the next one could come along and be slightly more detailed, thus expanding your understanding of Calvary by degrees. But thankfully, that is what makes the pattern so predictable. Because there are laws that govern its movement and growth, once you understand those foundational laws, you understand the pattern and how to recognize it. So again, without the foundation in place, the second lesson cannot move forward in your logic, much less if you're trying to figure it out seven or eight lessons down the road. It is for this very reason we find ourselves often asking, why did God do that?

So you can't miss the intended lesson of the flood. To do so would be like missing the concept behind the blood of Christ. Because if you don't see a value in that blood, then you fail to understand that it was the payment for our sins; and if that happens, the entire Bible becomes just another book on mythology. That makes all those blood sacrifices leading up to Calvary senseless pagan worship, and Jesus was just another good guy that was killed for all the wrong reasons. Why die if it's not important, right? Why shed your blood if it was never going to change the outcome of anything? You see, not knowing why He had to die takes away the power behind His death and robs Calvary of its most important asset, "the blood." If that happens, if it ceases to be seen as the "precious blood of Christ" and becomes common to us, then He died for nothing and our faith is in vain. It would literally make the entire event insignificant and quite ineffectual at saving anyone from their sins, and so the same holds true for the flood. It is as equally important as the blood.

Now, I know that may come as a shock to some hard-line blood-only believers, but that's because this flood is symbolically tied to the burial of the Christ. As I said before, the two events are intertwined. If the blood of a lamb can be symbolic of the blood of Christ, then the flood can be symbolic of His burial. Look, I know it's easy to see that the blood is the most important aspect of the whole process because it was the currency that bought our sins, but think about it for a minute. If He was never buried, then there could be no liberation of those souls from captivity, and there certainly would be no taking the keys of death, hell, and the grave. Moreover, we would lose the most important aspect to the whole event, which is that there could be no *resurrection.*

So I'm sorry, but each phase is as important as the other one; they are equal in their value. Leave one out, and Calvary loses it power. It simply won't work. It's like having a car with no gas: Everything is there to make it go, but without the fuel, you're stuck. They work together to get you to your destination; one without the other is useless. So you see, the Christ had to be buried just as much as He had to die and be resurrected. The things He would accomplish and the things He would destroy in that burial were paramount to the destruction of sin. I don't think I can stress this fact enough—The flood, the blood, and the resurrection are all built on one another, they are equally important, and they work together to the completion of this process we call Calvary.

So Alice, if you're ready to follow me a little deeper down this rabbit hole. I'll show you why the flood worked the way it did and why it was just as much a physical rebirth of humanity as it was a symbolic one. I'll also show you why God would choose to use water throughout the entire course of the Bible based on this one event. It is a journey that will forever change the way you see the first days of creation and the Bible, but keep in mind, this journey is not to change the system or the structure of the Bible. Rather, it is to organize our concepts of the system not only in which God constructed the Bible but also in nearly everything we see. So, forgive me if I get a little long long winded here, but we are about to breach a concept that has never really been discussed before, at least in modern times. In fact, the only place I have ever found anyone touching on the creation's true meaning was with John Milton, and that was the late 1700s.

In the Beginning

Now, the concept I'm talking about here was in our opening quote by Milton, where he wrote that God had made the earth pregnant in its beginning. I know it sounds far-fetched at first, but hear me out, because this is the primary reasoning behind the flood and the setting-up of the entire concept of being born again. So as we know when something conceives, it creates a womb around the fetus to protect it. But did you know that the same process holds true for the creation of the earth? Under closer inspection of the first days of creation, we see that this very thing is happening on day two. There, we find that God created a literal womb around the earth to protect it and mature it in its pregnancy. Now, I'm sure you're asking where? Well, before we get to that, let me first start by tearing down Milton's quote concerning the creation of the earth; it will help to set up the explanation.

Now, Milton said, "You (God) from the first was present, and with mighty wings outspread, dove like sat brooding on the vast abyss, and made it pregnant." What Milton was referring to was that first day of creation where the Bible said:

> In the beginning God created the heavens and the earth. The earth was without form, and void; and darkness was on the face of the deep. And the Spirit of God was hovering over the face of the waters. (Genesis 1:1–2)

So several things were happening here on that opening day, some of which were physical and some of which were spiritual, but all were foreshadows of things to come. For example, let's look at the reference to the Spirit of God hovering over or overshadowing something. That word hovering in the Hebrew means "to brood," as in a hen over her eggs, waiting for them to hatch. This makes perfect sense because we find that there are only two places in the entire Bible where this phenomenon occurs: The first of which is here in the beginning of creation and the other occurrence is found in another beginning, when God overshadowed the womb of the Virgin Mary and begun the life of the Christ.

> The Holy Spirit will come upon you, and the power of the Highest will **overshadow you**; therefore, also, that Holy One who is to be born will be called the Son of God. (Luke 1:35)

Like the rib from Adam's side, this day one moment was merely a foreshadowing of future events. When God was hovering over Mary, it was just as He did with the virgin earth in its beginning. He was creating life and the dream of a bride from a then-barren world, just as He would do with the womb of Mary. The birth of Christ would simply be that dream coming to fruition, the final step in attaining that bride and the dream that He so patiently waited on. But more importantly, what we learned here is that this event displayed how God would design and create through the birthing process. This day one was just the tipping of His hand; He was giving us a peek behind the veil.

Moreover, both of these examples would be creation moments, defining the two men that would forever change the course of an entire planet. The first was Adam, and the second one was Christ; the first man was formed from the earth, born on that sixth day, thus the symbol of the physical aspect of man. The second man was from the Spirit, miraculously conceived in the womb of Mary, thus symbolizing man's spiritual side. It is a perfect display of the dual nature that lies in every one of us and a symbol of the constant war between our flesh and our spirit. So you see, those first days of creation were ultimately just an allegorical representation of the Christ and how He would be born out of purity and nothingness. Once again, if Jesus was the lamb slain from the foundation of the world, then His birth would have also been planned from the foundation. You need to understand that everything that was done was done with Him in mind, which makes everything interconnected.

Turning now to the physical aspect of this phenomenon, we can begin to see that this day one was the actual beginning of life as we know it on earth; it would be the true Genesis point, in both a literal and Biblical sense because, at that moment, God was preparing to speak or place the seeds of creation into the earth. In the next verse, we find the actual placement of them, when God said, "Let there be light." Now, this was not light in the sense of the absence of darkness, the 186,000 miles per second light that we are used to; but this was a spiritual light; it was a life-giving light. If this were the actual sunlight, then what did He create on the fourth day when He said:

> Let there be lights in the firmament of the heavens to divide the day from the night; and let them be for signs and seasons, and for days and years; and let them be for lights in the firmament of the heavens **to give light on the earth**; and it was

so. Then God made two great lights: the greater light to rule the day (the sun), and the lesser light to rule the night (the moon). He made the stars also. God set them in the firmament of the heavens **to give light on the earth**, and to rule over the day and over the night, and to **divide the light from the darkness**. And God saw that it was good. So the evening and the morning were the **fourth day**. (Genesis 1:14–19)

So as you see, this day one light was not the sunlight, but it was a spiritual light. It was the kind of light that only a deity could express into a lifeless planet, the kind of light that would display a deeper hidden meaning to all things; it was the light that was to be the spark of life, which was needed to bring to life an otherwise inert planet. This was the only light that could drive out chaos and bring order, and this was the only light that could sustain the earth with its essence until the sun could be created.

This is why the Bible said on the first day and on the fourth that He "divided the light from the darkness." God was bringing order; He didn't divide two physical lights on two different days. What would be the point of that? No, but on that first day, He was dividing the light of life from the darkness of nothingness and thus creating a clear division between the two by placing the seeds of His light, giving DNA of creation into the womb of an otherwise barren planet. It was the injection of information that the planet needed to begin the creation process, and there is even a deeper allegorical meaning here concerning the barren wombs of women in the Bible, which we will get to if there is time. But with that, we begin to see that God was working on many different levels that first day, so many in fact that it is hard for us to really grasp everything that was happening, and perhaps, that's why no one has ever really spoken about this. It's just too complex.

As for now, just know that there was a spiritual separation of light on day one and a physical separation of light on day four:

> And God saw the light, that it was good; and
> God divided the light from the darkness. God
> called the light Day, and the darkness He called
> Night. So the evening and the morning were the
> first day. (Genesis 1:3–5)

Light and life, they are one and the same with God, as energy and mass were to Einstein and his equations.

So then, when God spoke on day one and said, "Let there be light," He was, in a very Prometheus-like moment of creation, placing His actual, physical DNA into the earth and becoming the Engineer of everything. In that moment, He became Saint Thomas's Prime Mover. But unlike the movie, God had no need to sacrifice Himself for the sake of creation. No, Elohim only needed to speak His DNA into the mineral-rich waters of the earth, thus fusing it with the earth's fertile organic materials to make it pregnant with the fetus of what would become the dry land and ultimately all of creation.

It would be the spark of life and the enrichment of information that this barren planet needed to get started and to become the mother of us all. But then, that begs the question, how do we know that it was God that did it and not some distant aliens as most think? Good question; in fact, it's such a good question that it bears such a relevance on our study that we need to take the time here and explain it. It will also help set up some future explanations in the book as to why God did what He did.

DNA

Now, if you didn't know, nearly every living thing on the earth possesses DNA. From humans to viruses, from plants to bacteria, its presence is in nearly everything organic. And, though complicated, DNA's basic function is the storage and transmission of biological information. So that means it not only tells our bodies how to form but also tells it if we'll have blue eyes or brown or if we'll be tall or short. It is the regulator of not only our lives but also everything that carries DNA. In fact, if you look close enough, you'll see that DNA governs our entire existence here on earth by keeping things in an organic order. Modern science says that there shouldn't be any order at all, but rather, that it is all by random natural selection. Yet they never can seem to explain just where that information for construction came from that tells DNA to do what it does. To them, it's known as "the origin of information enigma."

It is an enigma because DNA is a purely biosynthetic organism; this means that something living took organic compounds and used those to create DNA. Hence, the term bio means organic and synthetic, meaning created. And for something or someone to create on that level is simply mind-boggling. How does one store information in every living cell that instructs each little protein and element to even form a single strand of DNA? In short, DNA is creation in its purest form, and it lives inside each and every cell of our bodies. Dr. Stephen Myers of the Discovery Institute called the interworking of our cells "nanotechnology." That's because DNA is the engine of our entire creation; it's like a nanofactory working within each cell of our bodies, and modern science is now beginning to find out that this organic marvel is the perfect storehouse for information. In fact, they say that it's so perfect that many of them have now begun to believe that it is definitely engineered. Which brings us back to our former question, by whom, God or aliens?

Of course, I'm going to say by God, but it's my job to prove to you that it was by God and not aliens, but that will take more than this chapter to do so. So what we touch on here will just be the foundation of its biblical meanings and uses. But as we move deeper into these explanations, the more you'll begin to see that it was in fact this Hebrew God we call Elohim who created our DNA. But, at this point, it really doesn't matter to me if you believe it was done by aliens, just as long as people stop believing and teaching evolutionism.

Now in part, what helped me come to this conclusion was an article written by *Discovery News* about our human DNA and its possible link to being manufactured. The title of the article was *Is an alien message imbedded in our genetic code?* That was enough to peak my interest, and so I examined the article with much curiosity:

> The answer to whether or not we are alone in the universe could be right under our nose, or, more literally, inside every cell in our body. Could our genes have an **intelligently designed "manufacturer's stamp"** inside them, written eons ago elsewhere in our galaxy? Such a "designer label" would be an indelible stamp of a master extraterrestrial civilization that preceded us by many millions or billions of years. As their ultimate legacy, they recast the Milky Way in their own biological image (you have no idea how true that is).
>
> Vladimir I. shCherbak of al-Farabi Kazakh National University of Kazakhstan, and Maxim A. Makukov of the Fesenkov Astrophysical Institute, hypothesize that an intelligent signal embedded in our genetic code would be a mathematical and semantic (the study of meaning) message **that cannot** be accounted for by Darwinian evolution. They call it "biological SETI."
>
> Writing in the journal Icarus, they assert: "Once fixed, the code might stay unchanged over cosmological timescales; **in fact, it is the most durable construct known. Therefore it represents an exceptionally reliable storage for an intelligent signature**. Once the genome is appropriately rewritten **the new code with a signature will stay frozen in the cell** and its progeny, which might then be delivered through space and time."
>
> To pass the designer label test, any **patterns** in the genetic code must be highly statistically significant and possess intelligent-like features that are inconsistent with any natural known

process, say the authors. They go on to argue that in their detailed analysis, the human genome displays a **thorough precision-type orderliness** in the mapping between DNA's nucleotides and amino acids. "Simple arrangements of the code reveal an **ensemble** (a group producing a single effect) **of arithmetical and ideographical patterns of symbolic language** (which is a graphic symbol that represents an idea or concept)." They say this includes the use of decimal notation, logical transformations, and the use of the abstract symbol of zero. "Accurate and systematic, these underlying patterns appear as a product of **precision logic and nontrivial computing**," they assert.

It seems modern science is starting to catch on to what one of the codiscovers of DNA, Francis Crick, had come to realize a long time ago—The chemicals in DNA function like letters in a written language or digital symbols in a section of computer code. Crick said, "It is, in a sense, the key to molecular biology because it shows how the great polymer **languages**, the nucleic acid **language** and the protein **language**, are linked together." The keyword there is language. Where did that information come from, where did DNA learn that language, or how was that language encoded into its structure? Do you really think that proteins and nucleic acids just came up with their own language through random selection, really?

Once mankind realizes that this language was placed there by a higher power to form our organic lives, the debate between random chance and creation will finally be settled. Again, Stephen Myers addresses the heart of the question when he said, "The crucial question that will decide the debate about biological origins, is precisely the question of **the origin of information**, if you don't have instructions, if you don't have information, you can't build anything in life."

So you see, when God said, "Let there be light or life," it wasn't a metaphorical or symbolic placement of His DNA into the earth; but it was, in fact, quite literal in every way; and understanding the process by which He placed it there is half the battle because it is a true window into the creation process and a furtherance of not only the Bible but also our understanding of where we truly come from. And so naturally to see the next step in the process of creation for the earth, one only has to look to our own reproduction process to see how this is going to evolve because we ourselves are modeled after this creation pattern.

Just as it took a male and a female to create you and me, so it would take God the father and our earthly mother to begin creation. I like to think of it as if God was courting the universe looking for that one special planet that would become the womb of His creation. When He found it, He would consummate the marriage by speaking His DNA into this new bride, hence bringing a barren and dormant world to life. In that moment, when God placed His genetic code in the earth, He was combining it with the elements of this mother to aid Him in the creation of this new world.

When the information was combined with the organic materials, they would fuse together to become the building blocks of every living thing. By doing so, God was preparing the earth for the creation of Adam and all living creatures. Those waters and, most importantly, the clay would have been rich with the combination of divine DNA and maternal minerals, thus preparing it for God to reach down into that clay on the sixth day and form the creation that was going to be in His image.

As I said before, this concept is not a new one. The ancient peoples had similar stories; I believe I once read somewhere in the *Chronicles of Gilgamesh* that the gods had poured their blood into the clay of the earth to form man. That doesn't sound so far-fetched now. At one time, it would have been considered heresy, but you understand that the people of that era had no way of knowing what DNA was, but they understood what blood was, and that, in my book, is pretty close.

Now the Babylonians were not the only ones who had a creation story concerning blood; the Ancient Greeks have a similar account concerning the goddess Gaia, who was among the protogenos or primordial deities that were among the first entities or beings that came into existence. They believed that one day, Gaia formed an iron sickle and gave it to her sons to take vengeance upon their father Uranus who hated them. It was Cronos who took up the task and slew his father Uranus. And as the story goes, the drops of blood that fell from him upon the earth became the seeds of a new subset of gods and ultimately humanity. So I ask you again, is it so far-fetched to think that God actually placed His DNA into the earth in order to form Adam from the clay?

So then how do we know this combining of materials between mother and father actually happened in this way? Well, let's start with the earth. Did you know there are approximately 118 known elements in the earth, fifty-nine of which are found in the human body? Now I know that 98 of which are naturally occurring and the remaining 20 are synthesized, but that still means that exactly 50% of the earth's elements are inside each and every human. Combine that with our engineered DNA and you have a very passable fusion of materials between both our parents, where the elemental half is coming from mother earth, who supplied the building materials for life, and the other half coming from God, who supplied the design and information by which we would be built. If you ask me, it is a clear combination of the two coming together to create life, as all of nature does. As God said, "Let us make man in our image, after our likeness" (Genesis 1:26)

God couldn't have done it without the earth's help, at least in making a physical creation. I'm sure anything ethereal would have been quite simple, but something physical was going to take some organic materials and some complex engineering to boot. This was the process that began everything for us; it is the very process that has transcended time, passing down through the generations all the way to today; and again, thanks to science, we can now see the combined efforts of our Heavenly Father and earthly mother, fusing their biological information to create life; "and the light shined in the darkness"; and the nothingness could not comprehend it.

So you see, whether you believe it was God or aliens, it still took two parents donating their biological material for the cause of man. Besides, I cannot imagine how or where else this information could have been placed into the planet other than day one. Day one was the inception moment for everything. Even if it was extraterrestrials, day one is day one; it all had to start somewhere and some way, and this is the most plausible explanation. I mean you do realize that without DNA, there is nothing, and there can be nothing. It is the building blocks of our entire organic world.

And if you want to pin this on aliens, then in truth, isn't God alien to this planet? I mean He's not from here. By definition, alien means something foreign too. So that would make Him an alien to this planet even though He is our Father. Perhaps, He's the alien people are really all looking for, but they are too afraid to admit it. If He is real, then there is a lot of morality that goes along with that admission. I personally don't believe it was anything but God; simply because the Bible is one of the few places found that records the Maker's involvement with man throughout history, and it's also the only source that contains the definite mathematical patterns that deal with our creation, of which we will get to.

The Firmament

So at this point, God had made the earth pregnant by mingling His genetic material with that of the earth's, combining them together in the fashion that a woman conceives and thus began the second phase of the process, the formation of a protective barrier around this new life. And so begins day two of creation, as God said:

> Let there be a **firmament in the midst of the waters, and let it divide the waters from the waters.** Thus God made the firmament, and **divided the waters which were under the firmament from the waters which were above**

the firmament; and it was so. And God called
the firmament Heaven. So the evening and the
morning were the second day. (Genesis 1:6–8)

So question one, what's a firmament? Well, Webster's describes
it as "the vault or arch of the sky's, or the heavens." It is that expanse
or a space that exists between us and outer space; and, in our reading
here, it means that God took the waters of the earth and pulled them
apart, separating them, thus leaving some on the earth and placing
some in the heavens, literally "dividing the waters from the waters,"
encapsulating the earth and creating the same outer barrier of protection that an embryo experiences in the first moments of conception,
which is known as a gestational sac. What's a gestational sac? Well,
it's a large cavity of fluid that is created in the beginning of what
doctors call the embryogenesis. During this phase, a sac is formed
around the embryo from the maternal plasma, which is simply the
fluid portion of the blood. It is then separated from the amniotic sac
through osmotic and hydrostatic pressure, turning the gestational sac
into an additional burrier around the amniotic sac to further aid in
the protection of the fetus.

Conception

So on day two, God literally took the earth's waters and separated them through hydrostatic force, creating a gestational-like sac
of maternal plasma from the waters of the earth, hence the phrase
"divide the waters from the waters." Why would He need to create
a layer of protection around the earth? Well, some have surmised
that it was to protect this new planet from harmful cosmic radiation
that would come from the creation of the soon to be new sun. But
what I find interesting about the whole thing is how much it imitates
a woman's first few days following conception. And why not, why
wouldn't He begin the creation of the earth like that of a woman?

After all, we are just smaller replications of His creation model;
we all exist between the macro- and the microcosm. How a woman
conceives and carries a child was not by happenchance; it is purely by

design, and the first few days of creation reflect that. But let me show you what I mean because sometimes, a picture is worth a thousand words. If we take an image of what the gestational sac looks like and the internals it protects, it appears in this fashion:

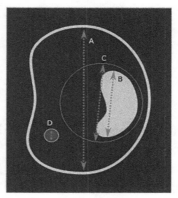

A, gestational sac (GS); B, crown-rump length
(CRL) of embryo; C, amniotic sac; D, yolk sac

Now, translate that image to fit our discussion so that the notes from this image can be interpreted like this. The space between C and A is the firmament, and A is the waters above, and B would be the land mass, or Pangea, as it was called when it was all one piece, which would be formed on the third day. As for C, it would be the earth itself and the waters below, or the amniotic sac that protects the new fetus. And as for D, it is the yolk sac or as it is better known today as the umbilical vesicle; its purpose is to transfer nutrients that aid in the embryo's growth, much in the same way the moon transfers gravity to the earth, to aid in its growth and stabilization.

Now, concerning that land mass, if we take a look at a proposed map of what Pangea would have appeared like in that beginning, we find it is strikingly similar to that of B, the image of the crown-rump length resting inside of that sphere, or amniotic fluid sac, which is the embryo itself.

So is it a coincidence that the formation of the earth in its beginnings was like that of a woman conceiving and forming an embryo? Or that the landmass known as Pangea is strikingly similar to that of the crown-rump length of a newly forming embryo? And how about the landmass appearing on the third day—Is it too far-fetched to see it as the result of the two parents' union, just like you and I when were formed in our mother's womb by the union of our biological parents?

No, of course not. If God created all of this, then why would He change His design for conception and creation? The woman conceives and creates life the same way God did it and designed it from the beginning; this is why John Milton said that in the beginning, God made the earth pregnant. So was it possible that Milton knew all of this? Of course not. He had no way of knowing how this process worked, nor did science have any idea of how an embryo was even formed or that DNA even existed at that time. Science had not yet caught up with the concept of this, but Milton understood it in its metaphorical sense. He understood the implied concept of the allegory, and that was really all he needed. But now with the help of modern science, we can look through that allegorical microscope and see what Milton could not see. We can see the true physical aspect of creation; and, by doing so, we as believers begin to move from the realms of speculation to those of knowing. Again, it is all about knowing why. It is where the only true power lies.

So thanks to science, we can now see those six days of creation with a little more depth and clarity. It helps us to see that it was also a foreshadow for the very process of biological reproduction. Nearly everything biological comes into this world via a womb of some sort, from eggs, to cocoons, to trees and the fruit they bear; even viruses use the host cell as a womb to birth its offspring. Take an orange, for example. If you look at it closely, you'll see that it is a womb, with its outer skin acting as the gestational sac and the meat of the orange is acting as the inner amniotic fluid sac that holds the seeds, which are the embryos of a future life, and the stem supplies the nutrients just like the umbilical cord of the mother. Everything shares in the gift of design and birth.

It's all an endless cycle of dropping those wombs to the ground and letting them die. In that death, though, a new seed is able take root, and the orange is born again. They're all just wombs holding the future creation within themselves, in hopes that the species might live on through that rebirth. And here is that great mystery partially answered, when Jesus told Nicodemus, "Nicodemus you must be born again" (John 3:3). He should have understood that everything goes through the circle of life if it is to continue on; the Christ had to die, all so that He could live forever; and so, in like fashion, we must also die metaphorically, in order to be born again and have the opportunity to live forever. It has always been this way because it was engineered to be just that, and no one is ever going to get to God other than experiencing a rebirth. As for the rest of this mystery, we will address it later on.

It should be easy to see that God does nothing out of order. How many times have we seen those documentaries or school videos where it is one successive birth after another from any number of animals or insects or flowering plants? Do you really think that's Darwinism, really? You want me to believe that a bananas DNA just randomly chose the right sequence to create that fruit and then just stopped its selection process when it became a banana? Why not go on? Why has it not evolved further?

It certainly doesn't look like random evolution to me. It looks more like intelligent design—like something or someone engineered a process for reproduction and placed it into everything organic. Sure, it may come in different forms and packages; but, in essence, they are still at the core all the same. Everything organic shares in that common process; we all come from some sort of a womb. It is the well of information that we all draw from, from plants to humanity; the design is literally forcing us to share in the mathematical pattern that is transmitted through DNA. That's why everything that has DNA reproduces much in the same way. It has all been designed by the same designer; once you find something that works, why change?

So I ask you, could all of this just be happenchance? Could this much order and design just from a purely DNA perspective, come from a big bang? There's no way. It's all too perfect. There are too many exacts that exist in the earth and in the universe to believe in that. Even if you look at it from a purely logically and statistical perspective, it ultimately leaves you asking the question how could all of this just happen? I mean really, how could all of these complex designs and storehouses of information come into existence out of nothing? Do you really think it was random evolution? You understand that the odds of that actually working are somewhere in the neighborhood of 1 in $10^{41,000}$ power? That's a number that is larger than the partials in our universe. Or do you think it was an intelligent designer, whose intellect is far beyond our comprehension?

I could go on here with exacts, in the earth, in our universe, or in our environment; but we would run out of time and room. How can anyone not see that there is a definite pattern to all of this, that there is something ordering everything right down to our very cell structure? If you don't believe me, just wait until we get to the mathematical portion, because you will then.

So it shouldn't be hard for anyone to see that all of creation shares in this common process of combining elements with DNA to create a womb. Those that still deny are simply intellectually dishonest. But I think for the majority of us it hasn't been so much the fact that we didn't believe that there was a designer because somewhere, buried deep down inside, we have always known it was this way; I think the real problem has been our inability to combine faith and science to properly explain how all of this works. I think it's quite sad that some believe that the two cannot be intermingled, but that's really for the ignorant, isn't it? For those blind faithful who are on either side of the proverbial fence, who sadly pledge that blind obedience more to the structure than to the truth.

Science is constantly producing new truths about us and our universe every day, so we cannot discard everything they say just because someone doesn't believe in God. All of their discoveries should point us to a designer, to the ultimate scientist; if we can't find the connection, it's not their fault, but ours. So why reject the information that science gives us if we truly have a Promethean-like engineer for a god? We should find Him in everything we do, simply by the consistent patterns that are in nature alone. You realize that you cannot have consistent patterns without a designer behind them, how else could everything natural have so much in common with these first few verses of scriptures and the birthing process, unless it is all engineered?

In fact, with their help and research, we are going to give the Bible a new life, by giving explanations to things that formerly had none, in turn giving us a greater understanding of the whys. So then, that should leave us with just one clear path to follow concerning science, and that is we must borrow from their research to prove our biblical theories. The information is there. We just need to connect the dots, right? Not convinced? Well, let me show you what I mean because we are not done with this outer layer of water just yet. Let's borrow from someone else's work to give us a better understanding of this earthly womb.

Now, believe it or not, there has been a great deal of research done on the existence of this outer layer of water. It's known as "water canopy theory" or the "water vapor canopy," and the researchers point to the fact that there was definitely something that surrounded the earth in those formative years. They also say that this canopy would've remained in place from this second day of creation until the time of Noah when that canopy finally broke.

Not wishing to drag this out, I'll give you the condensed version. Quoting from answersingenesis.org concerning this topic, they say:

After God finished making all the plants and animals during Creation Week, the Bible says, "The Lord God **had not** caused it to rain on the earth, and there was no man to till the ground; but **a mist went up from the earth** and watered the whole face of the ground (Genesis 2:5–6)." So no rain--just a mist or dew.

Later, God told Noah during the 600th year of his life that He would "**cause it to rain** on the earth forty days and forty nights" (Genesis 7:4) Noah may have faced new weather conditions during and following the Flood that he had never experienced before, but just what was the nature of these changes? It seems clear that he saw a rainbow for the first time. And he was assaulted by severe weather of a magnitude never seen on earth before or since.

Dr. Dillow, and Dr. Vardiman, and others have suggested that the vapor canopy created on the second day caused a greenhouse effect before the Flood with a pleasant sub-tropical-to-temperate climate all around the globe, even at the poles where today there is ice. This would have caused the growth of lush vegetation on the land all around the globe. The discovery of coal seams in Antarctica containing **vegetation** that is not now found growing at the poles, but which obviously grew under warmer conditions, was taken as support for these ideas.

So in Genesis 7:11 the reference to the windows of heaven being opened has been interpreted as the collapse of such a water vapor canopy, which somehow became unstable and fell as rain. **Volcanic eruptions** associated with the breaking

up of the fountains of the great deep could have
thrown dust into the water vapor canopy, causing
the water vapor to nucleate on the dust particles
and make rain.

So you see, when God created this canopy on day two, He did
it to create a greenhouse effect over the entire planet, which in turn
would protect the planet from possible cosmic radiation from the
new sun and accelerate the growth process of all organic materials,
just like a fetus developing in its mother's womb, being suspended
and protected in that maternal plasma. So from a scientific perspective, the canopy was acting as an incubator, the same as the gestational sac of a woman. It was put in place to speed up the embryotic
growth process for the earth within it. That's why researchers have
found greenery in the coal seams of the Antarctic; the entire earth
was in the hothouse of a literal womb. And since we are talking about
science and design on a grander scale here, then why wouldn't one
make all organic creation function the same way? I mean, if a process
or pattern is found that works, why change it? Why make the creation of the earth any different than that of the design of a woman's
ability to conceive, or vice versa?

Remember it is engineering we're talking about here; be it
mechanical or organic, it really doesn't matter because, usually, once
an engineer or architect finds a design they like, they very rarely
change it. One only has to look as far as some of the premier archi-
tects in the world to see that principle in action, such as those like
Frank Lloyd Wright and his modern organic designs, Le Corbusier
and his use of proportions, or Amanda Levetes and her unbeliev-
ably beautiful organic designs. If you study them, you'll see that
they never really changed from their original design concepts. Why?
Because once they brought that vision to life that was in their minds,
why change? To them, it is perfect.

Besides, it is human nature not to change. People as a whole
love predictability and patterns; and, if we love them, how much
more does God? After all, is not human nature merely an extension
of godly nature? So I ask again, why would we be made any different

in our creation process if everything derives from "One" designer, who created one binary driver for everything, called DNA? The simple answer is we're not because God is the architect, DNA is the blueprint, and the earth's organic materials are the building blocks and mortar that are used to create the design. So why would He change the design if it is already perfect? As the old saying goes, "if it's not broke, don't fix it," right?

Birth

So then if God designed both the earth and us to be just alike in pregnancy, then the earth should have possessed the same attributes as us, like being carried for a term and delivering at the end of that term. What I mean is, if a woman carries a child for a term of nine months, then the earth should have had a term limit as well. If it was truly carried for a term, then it should have by that same design went through birth pains just as we do to deliver said infant. And so it did. You see, those volcanic eruptions that Dr. Dillow and Dr. Vardiman wrote about happened for a reason; not only would they have served to break up the land mass known as Pangea, but also they would have been acting as the labor pains of a woman, sending their hot volcanic ash into the atmosphere like contractions, thus causing the water canopy to condense or contract and ultimately break, like that of a woman's when her waters break.

So these volcanic eruptions and this oncoming flood were simply the earth's term coming to an end. Just like a tree dropping its fruit, the earth was about to give birth. What was she going to birth? She was about to give birth to Noah for the second time in his life; only this time, it would be symbolic for him and very literal for the earth, thus exposing both Noah and the earth to a new environment without the protection of the canopy. It should make perfect sense that the earth was in its gestational period from that second day on, maturing and growing like a fetus inside that womb of water until it reached an age and a level of maturity where it was ready to be birthed.

And while we're here, let me explain Pangea and this breaking up and drifting apart. Because you do realize that to separate the continents as much as they are today, you would need much more time than the current six-thousand-year religious view. At the rate they move now, to achieve the current distance, it would be in the neighborhood of 100,000 plus years. But those continents could have been separating long before that apocalypse; it perhaps merely speed up the process. Besides, no one has an accurate estimation on the time between when the dry land was formed on the third day and the actual flood, meaning it could have been a literal day for each day of creation, or it could have been, as the Jews call this area of the scripture, concerning the time between the days, an epoch of time. That simply means that it is longer than an era and can cover more than one lifetime or even an eon, and I only mention this because I don't want to be ignorant to the facts that are before us, and that is the issue of time and separation. The only other plausible answer is that the flood was such a violent event that it literally caused a sort of a hyperfracturing between the continents. I'm simply offering one possible solution to a much larger question, which I have my own theories on, but we don't have the time or the room for them in this book.

Types and Shadows

But my point is that the life of Noah and this flood were designed to symbolize Christ and Calvary. As I said before, for Noah, this was going to be just as much a spiritual rebirth as it was a physical one; and of course, it was all done through the use of water. This moment was no different than when God took out the rib of Adam's to create Eve; this Flood would simply be yet another look through time and a foreshadowing of what one day would come to pass. If we examine the similarities between the lives of Noah and Adam, we find that they are nearly identical. Where we see in both stories, each has a physical birth into life. For Adam, it was by God into the Garden; and, for Noah, it was by his mother into the post-Garden world. Then, we see in both cases that sin causes an expulsion from each place and a symbolic death. For Adam, it was his sin that caused the expulsion from the Garden, and the symbolic death was being cast out from said Garden in the wake of those sacrifices. In Noah's case, it was the sins of the world that drove him out and into the Ark, which upon entering was a symbol of his death and the flood was the burial.

Moreover, we see that it was divine intervention that delivered each of them into two very opposing physical and symbolic worlds. In Adam's case, it was into the harshness of the wilderness; and, in Noah's case, it was into a very thinly shadowed symbolic promised land that was free from sin. This is a very common biblical theme, transitioning from one phase of life to another as when the children of Israel left Egypt and, again, a very distant image of the born again process.

The only real difference between the two stories lies in the typesetting, where we see in Adam's case that the primary delivering factor for him was the shedding of blood to set the type of Christ's death. As for Noah, his type delivering factor would be the water, acting as the tomb, thus allowing him to be born again from certain death. And here in part is why blood and water flowed from the side of Christ; it was to symbolize the process in which God brought about the actual event of Calvary and to prove that He was the Christ that came by blood and water, as did all those before Him. As John wrote, "This is He who came by water and blood—Jesus Christ; not only by water, but by water and blood. And it is the Spirit who bears witness, because the Spirit is truth" (1 John 5:6).

The whole process brings to mind the riddle of Samson, "Out of the eater, something to eat; out of the strong, something sweet" (Judges 14:14). Out of death came life, and out of what was never to be overcome, the strength of the grave, something sweet overcame it: Jesus. So you see, the two events were just parallels of each other, only where Noah's life operated in the symbolism of Calvary, Christ was in the actual. And the primary lesson here was not that God would punish mankind and start over again, but that this outer layer of water was created to mimic a womb and, in doing so, allowed the earth to experience a literal birth, or rebirth. All so God could create an example for us to follow when the Christ would come and experience His death, burial, and resurrection, or rebirth, all to save mankind. In fact, if this flood never happened, then Jesus would have never uttered that famous line, "Nicodemus, you must be born again" (John 3:3). That whole concept began right here with the flood and then was built upon type after type, and shadow after shadow, until the day came where Jesus could make that statement so confidently to Nicodemus.

God doesn't just work on a single level at a single time, but there are layers to His designs and processes. There is always a much deeper meaning hiding just beneath the surface. And I'll admit, seeing and explaining the allegorical side is not always the easiest thing to do because it often requires a much more in-depth explanation. Putting things in an easy application is often difficult because that profound allegorical explanation is usually found in that strange place where our logical minds come in contact with the illogical spiritual side of things, where rationality dissolves and gives way to the unexplainable almost dreamlike metaphors of the Bible. It's a difficult place where we try to put the deep allegorical meanings of the Bible in terms that we can all understand and believe. As Mark Twain once said on the topic of truth, "Truth is stranger than fiction, but it is because fiction is obliged to stick to possibilities."

It is because of vast concepts like this that the literal and spiritual side of this womb has remained relatively untouched since the time of Milton. Understand that the explanations were just too difficult to extract at that time because they laid out there somewhere in the complexities of science in that place where the extremely complex spiritual and allegorical designs of God's are almost overwhelming for our minds; and, yet, oddly enough, how simple they become once you are on the other side of it. However, understanding that God never works on a single level is half the battle. The architect of the entire universe was always working on multiple levels, setting types and foundation stones, all so we could have something to build our faith and salvation on.

René Descartes had once put learning like this, and I'm paraphrasing, "There is no squabbling in math, because were taught a fundamental truth in the beginning and then we build on that truth to the next level." That's all we are doing here—We are learning the basics, building them to Christ, building them to the full revelation of who He was and what He accomplished. But sadly too many of us have been taken straight to Christ, bypassing the fundamental lessons of the Bible and going straight to the advanced lessons. This is why so many of us have been left asking the question of why. And there's the crux of the matter. Not everyone is a blind follower; some of us want to know why and not be viewed as rebellious for it. So understand that you are just learning the fundamentals of the Bible and how to identify them and their values, its blood, then water, and then the miraculous. It is a death, then a burial, and then a resurrection. It is a simple mathematical equation, only in allegorical form, no different than learning how 2+2 works, and then moving on too more complex problems like $a^2 + b^2 = c^2$. Calvary was just God's equation to cure sin.

> The reasonable man adapts himself to the world; the unreasonable one persists in trying to adapt the world to himself. Therefore all progress depends on the unreasonable man. (George Bernard Shaw)

CHAPTER 4

❧

The Flood

Why Water

From water does all life begin. (Dune)

So just how did water get here on Earth? That seems to be the million-dollar question that is still perplexing scientists today. Why? The earth is a bit of a universal anomaly, as it is the only known planet that possesses liquid water. Of course, odds would indicate that there are others out there, seeing that there are about at current estimates 100 to 200 billion galaxies in the universe; but for now, it seems we are it. Yet, I still find it interesting that no one can really give us a definitive answer on just how it got here. Sure, there are a lot of theories out there, like ice comets hitting the earth in its formative years; but, until proven, they remain just that—a theory. Much like Einstein's gravitational wave theory, until recently proven to exist, it remained on that proverbial shelf of theories, right beside this one. Besides, if you consider the amount of water that is on Earth, which is about 3.661×10^{20} in gallons, it would take one heck of a lot of ice comets hitting the earth in those formative years to create that much water.

Now to be fair, even the Bible leaves it to the imagination because it was apparently already here when God arrived as well, as the Bible says, "The earth was without form, and void; and darkness was on the face of the **deep**. And the Spirit of God was hovering over the face of the **waters**" (Genesis 1:2). I think I even read in one rendering of the Bible where God asked Job, "Where were you when I **found** the Earth?" If that's true, if God just happened upon the earth after creating it eons ago and water was already here, then only one of two options exist. Either He created the earth with water in the beginning, or it accumulated over time. Nevertheless, from the Bible's rendering, all that God had to do was simply add the dry land and life. Now that's no small feat, mind you; but, by that logic, it seems that water was here long before He arrived. And yes, I know it says in the beginning God created the heavens and the earth, implying that water was created along with them; but it never outright mentions this key element of creation, nor do we have a clue as to when that beginning was.

Now, if that doesn't boggle your mind, then consider the fact that the water was in its liquid state when God arrived, not frozen, as it should have been with no sun. Remember that that wasn't coming until the fourth day. I have my own theories on the whole matter, but they are far too expansive for one chapter. But all theories aside, what is factual about water is that it seems to be the one element that we can all agree on, from evolutionists to creationists. All life came from it, and without it, life could not exist. There is no disputing that simple fact.

The more I study water, though, the more I realize that we are very much like Frank Herbert's fictional planet of Arrakis, because water is the most precious commodity on the entire planet whether we realize it or not. In fact, water is of such a vital importance to all living things on earth that in some organisms, up to 90% of their body weight is derived from water. Even the majority of our body weight as adults is composed of 60% water, with some organs possessing more and others less, as broken down by H. H. Mitchell in the *Journal of Biological Chemistry 158*: "The brain and heart are composed of 73% water, and the lungs are about 83% water. The skin contains 64% water, muscles and kidneys are 79%, and even the bones are watery: 31%." As you can see, humanity has put a lot of effort into understanding water and its importance; from theories of how it got here to even breaking it down to its molecular construction, man, it seems, has fully exploited water and its many uses, or has he? Oddly enough, it appears that no one has ever really considered the Bible and its water content or the importance it has in the processes that are carried out in it.

For example, if we take just the first seven days of creation, we find that day one and day two of which we have already spoken of almost entirely involved the use of water. And on day three, we see that water played a huge role when the dry land was called out of it. Then on day five, we find that God used it to create all the birds and the fish. So that's four out of seven days that water was directly used in the creation process; and, if you want to get technical, the last day of creation was a rest day, so you can mark that one off. Now, you have a majority; four out of six days that water was used in the creation process. In fact, day four, the day of light, was really the only day of construction that did not rely on the use of water because even when God created Adam's body from the clay on the sixth day, that body would have been composed of 60% water, right? So in reality, we see that in five out of six days, water played a major role in creation; and if you're keeping count, that is a number in percentage terms that is above 83%.

In short, no water, no life. And trust me, I understand that there are many other key elements that all factor into our existence, but there is none as important as water. And that to me is what makes Frank Herbert's simple statement so profound—"from water does all life begin"—because it forces our thoughts toward this one simple life-giving element in a way that most of us have taken for granted, and I'm not just talking about the role it plays in our everyday biology, but the one it plays in our religious lives as well. It seems that water holds the balance of all creation within its construction, reaching far beyond our biological lives and deep into our spiritual lives and beliefs. The same could be said for water from a biblical perspective as well. No water, no life.

Whether you know it or not, water permeates the entire Bible. It brings forth all life, in both the physical and spiritual realms. Water is the conveyance between lives and worlds and no human comes into this life unless it is by water. And so it is because of this wide-spread Biblical use that I believe water deserves not just another look, but an extensive tearing down. Why? For one, this is to help us better understand its true symbolic meanings and the context in which it was used throughout the Bible to the saving of God's elect. The other reason is to gain some insight into God's thinking because, up until now, we have all overlooked water and its importance to God. Besides, if we take the time now, then when we finally do get to Calvary, we will fully understand what it was accomplishing.

Now, I don't know how long it was from the birth of Adam until the flood. I've never really sat down and plotted out the years for myself, but I've read two accounts that said it could have been as many as 1650 years. If that's true, then it appears that God painstakingly waited to implement the next part of His plan, but then again, what's time to God? I think it was Peter who said, "A thousand years is like a day" to Him. But nevertheless, setting eternity aside and turning to thoughts, I used to think that God was waiting on a man to come before He brought the Flood, waiting on someone that could come in the symbolic form of His Christ and fulfill the next portion of the pattern.

I have since come to realize that it was in fact a collection of things. For one, it was timing. Those 1650 years were not arbitrary; He had a reason for starting on that date; and hopefully, we can get to it in this book. The other was design; this entire event was modeled after Calvary as were all things. And lastly, it was the man, who was to be the Christ for this allegory; he was the most important part of this equation, above even the timing and the design of God. Why? Because timing and design have no will of their own, but the man does. He was the one that was drawn there by God, in essence having his own will overridden so that he could play the part of the Christ and set the type. But rest assured, God was never waiting on the man. Everything was planned and predetermined from the beginning. Noah was just the forerunner in what would be a long line of Messiah figures to come until the actual one would arrive and fulfill all this symbolism. So he, just as they that would follow in his footsteps, would be the ones subject to the timing and design of

God, almost moving through the entire object lesson that they were involved in without a will of their own.

And again, I mention the word equation, simply because everything that God does is an expression of equality between quantities, be they literal or figurative, meaning that through the use of quantities, the allegory becomes a more concise way of expressing information symbolically. What the pattern does is give us the formula for solving the equation. As for the formulas themselves, they represent the general construct or conceptual ideals that are of a relationship between given quantities, which are typically subjective and not based on empirical evidence. Meaning that in each allegory, there is always a certain set of given quantities; be it blood, or water, or men and design, they are simply the elements that are used to create the quantities, which in turn are used to create the allegory. And once you define those quantities, you can create a formula to test and compare each allegory to see if it fits the pattern.

And this is the sum of my point that the quantities are so reliable that one could convert them into mathematical style equations, such as man would be (M), timing would be (T), design (D), and the sum of the figures would be the allegory (A). Put them together and you have your simplified allegorical equation, $M+T+D=A$. The allegories were simply His way of transmitting to us the solution to the problem of sin, which of course would one day be Calvary. They are the compiled formulas of God's thoughts and His shadowed intent for humanity's salvation, and through them, we see how He likes to operate and design in these definite equitable patterns. Be it through the symbolism of elements or people, or as in the case of the Ark and its mathematical elements, which is a wonderful display of a suballegory working within the major allegory, a clear case of God's use of the macro- and the microcosm within the same story—This is how He designs all of His allegories. There is always a subset of symbolism operating within the main symbolic story—They are plans within plans and wheels within wheels. That's just how He likes to design. If you don't believe me, ask Ezekiel.

But it is of some importance that you understand at least a portion of this process now so that later on, as it is unfolding in other places, you will recognize it and know it origins. You need to understand just how much God controlled the lives of the people that He was using. Why? Because this is yet another definite process that God never breaks from; you will see it time and again until the Christ. Another thing that you will notice about this process is that once the allegory was completed, the person that was being used quickly fades into the pages of obscurity. Why? Because God was done creating the pattern, the object lesson was over, and there was no need to use them any further. And that's simply because the Christ was only going to Calvary once; there would be no need to repeat the process. There were only a chosen few that ever got to be involved in more than one pattern setting, among them were the likes of Abraham and Moses, and of course, there was a reason for that.

But the whole process brings to mind what Paul wrote in Romans, "For whom He **foreknew**, He also **predestined** to be **conformed** to the image of His Son" (Romans 8:29). God foreknew this event and Noah long before He started this project, and He predestined or prearranged Noah's life and all those that would follow in his Messiah like footsteps to be modeled or conformed to the image of His Son's death, burial, and resurrection. What Christ did in the actual, they did in the allegory. So you see, Noah had no choice in the matter, even though we would like to think he did. His life was unknowingly and unavoidably set on a collision course with the next allegory. He was led to that one single point in time where the desire and design of God would come together to form His next vision of Calvary.

This coincidently is the very essence of what biblical events are born from. When you read the Bible through, you can't help but notice that it's always one man entering in at just the right time, in an almost superhero-like fashion to turn the tide and save the day through some divine miracle, thus delivering God's people from their impending doom. It is a common theme that in itself forms yet another pattern that you can find in nearly every major story—from Joseph ascending to power in Egypt just in time to save the then-known world from the famine to Moses's return from the wilderness just in time to deliver the Israelites from their slavery and the slaughter of their children to Joshua crossing the Jordan and leading the people from the barren wilderness into the Promised Land. And who can forget Elijah, who converted the entire backslidden nation of Israel by calling fire down from heaven when facing the 450 prophets of Baal? It is a typical Messiah pattern that was set in the image of Christ Himself, who took on the sins of the world to save humanity just in time.

Now, I don't expect you to see or understand it all right away, but as we progress through the book, you will see how God has woven everything together through these allegorical patterns, from nature to humanity, from His word to His Christ, merging them all in an equation-type fashion to be the very blueprints of mankind's salvation. Again, the allegories were just His way of expressing to us then the message of Calvary through the limited means of symbolism. None of these past events could have worked 100% at lifting the curse of death and curing us from sin because if they did, then why send the Christ? What would be so special about Him coming and doing the same thing? Nothing, I assure you.

No, all the allegory could do was placate the judgments of God until the actual substance of all those shadows could come to liberate us. However, don't doubt for one minute that they were anything less than the perfectly orchestrated events that God had wanted them to be. To say that there were no perfect shadows of Christ in the Old Testament is to imply that God Himself is not perfect. Again, each event was exactly what He wanted it to be; everything was ordered, even down to the length of time the events lasted. It's just that He could not display all of the attributes of Christ in one or two allegories. What man could have borne that kind of load? None, I assure you. And so it is for that reason that it would take so many men and events to paint for us the full picture of what Christ and Calvary would do for all of humanity. As I said before, God does nothing out of order, and the sooner you learn that, the sooner you'll see that these allegories stand as yet another proof that a much higher intelligence wrote the Bible.

Briefly moving back to water's meaning though, we should understand that the flood was not going to be a half-measure against sin, but rather an all-out assault. Why? Because the flood waters themselves would symbolize the level at which the mercy of God would one day flood into the world after the death of Christ to wash away the sins of humanity. I could not imagine a better element to symbolize the Mercy of God than water; it is a perfect elemental type, delivering a flawless symbolic quantity to the allegory, and one of the many reasons why God chose water in all of His allegorical settings. So understanding that, it's easy to see that by sheer reason of the symbolism alone the destructive force of the flood would have to be total, destroying everything that was tainted by the sins of humanity, save that which was in the Ark.

Now if you are curious like me, you probably have always wondered just how many people there were on the planet before the flood, simply so you can put that level of destruction into some perspective. Well, I did some poking around on what the population growth would have been like before the flood and found that, on the conservative side, it was about a billion people; and some have put the estimates as high as seven billion people! I know it sounds impossible, but they say that is in part due to the fact that people in general were living so much longer back then. It seems 900 years was the average; compound that with the 1650 years, and there you go. If you still don't believe me, then you need to explore Thomas Malthus's exponential growth model for humanity. The best version is the one where a single sheet of paper is folded multiple times until it reaches an unbelievable number in just a hundred folds. The simple jest of the lesson is that if humanity is allowed to keep doubling unchecked, it will reach exponential numbers. It is all quite staggering.

But when I saw that population number, my mind went racing; I never thought that there were that many people on the earth before the flood. It was simply mind-boggling to imagine that all those people were about to lose their lives. And to think that Noah was the only man living for God is an even a greater stretch of the imagination. I couldn't imagine being the only person on the planet following a certain way or belief, much less one in a billion plus. The pressure to go with the flow must have been enormous; I know we like to think of Noah as this strong stoic man, easily resisting the temptations of the day; but to be the only one must have been mentally crushing. You understand that having your will overridden by God is not always a clear-cut thing. Why? Because the contact with God on direction is not every day; it is sometimes decades before He speaks to you again, as in the case of Abraham. So the room to ponder if one is simply mad is tremendous. Yet the Bible did say that "Noah was a just man, **perfect** in his generations" (Genesis 6:9).

But still knowing that, I'm sure that he thought he was nuts a time or two while building that Ark. It had never rained before; why would it rain now? This must have been running on a continuous loop inside of his mind. You understand that there is a certain kind of madness that sets in when someone is isolated in such a way, and as if that were not enough, the Bible said that he preached to those people for over a hundred years while he was building the Ark. What an impossible task, literally a billion to one odds that he would have convinced anyone that a flood was coming, especially seeing that it had never rained before. That's like going to China and saying rice is bad for you; who is going to listen to you? Who in the world is going to stop eating rice in China? But, despite it all, it seems God has a way of calling that one man among the many who is so set in his mind that even madness and rejection cannot deter him from heralding God's message to the unhearing masses. Perhaps, this is the true reason why the Bible says, "Noah found grace in the eyes of the Lord" (Genesis 6:8).

Grace

Now, for those who don't fully understand what grace is, it is simply the unmerited or unearned favor of God. And that unearned favor fell on Noah—not because He lived unlike everyone else, but because he believed in what God had told him—and that belief or faith was counted unto Noah as righteousness or virtue. It would be the same gauge that was measured against Abraham, whereby he was called the father of the faithful because "he staggered not at the promise of God through unbelief," and that same kind of faith is what brought God's grace upon Noah. Yet for all of that grace,

Noah and his family were not out of trouble just yet because they still needed a way of escape.

Faith alone was not going to get them out of the coming destruction; Noah could have sat there a thousand years believing that an Ark was just going to appear, but that would have only gotten him killed like everyone else. No, there had to be some form of action on Noah's part. As James said, "Faith without works is dead" (James 2:26). God just wasn't going to do it all for him; Noah had to couple that faith and grace with the construction of the Ark. Why did it require some action? Because Calvary was going to require action. Don't get me wrong. It could never have been done without faith, for surely it was Noah's faith that brought him into the grace of God; but it was the grace of God that would produce a way of escape, which came in the form of the Ark. It was the righteous pattern or blueprint for salvation.

That's exactly what the Apostle Paul was talking about when he wrote, "For by **grace** you have been saved **through faith**, and that **not of yourselves**; it is the **gift of God**, **not of works**, lest anyone should boast" (Ephesians 2:8–10). Grace worked through the faith of Noah to produce the gift of the Ark. There was no way Noah could have ever conceived the idea of the Ark, nor would God have allowed him to use his own idea, "lest anyone should boast." His salvation would purely rely on God and His pattern of salvation, which came in the form of the Ark. That's what Paul meant when he wrote "not of yourselves" because there is nothing you or I could conceive or do to merit salvation. It is solely by the design of God, hence the Ark and all the other forms of deliverance He would use. Why? Because they were righteously conceived by God to be the symbolic forms of Calvary, which would one day save us all.

It is the use of these three quantities—faith, grace, and pattern—that produces the formula for salvation. Again creating an equation, we see that Faith (F) produces Grace (G) and Grace produces a Pattern (P) or a gift that becomes a way of escape and produces or sum of salvation (S): F+G+P=S. It is a natural biblical order of operation. And this too is another equation that never changes throughout the entire course of the Bible; you can find it from Abraham to Elijah to the Christ. It is God's equation for pulling those He loves out of the fires and floods of this world and sparing them from the judgments to come. You'll find it in every case if you look hard enough because it creates our pattern of Calvary.

Now, this is a perfect place to clear up what seems to be a bit of confusion concerning the grace and the mercy of God. Grace is the unmerited favor of God, and that unearned favor is what brings one to the point of salvation. It does not forgive someone of their sins. That is reserved for the mercy of God; it is the compassion or forgiveness shown toward someone whom it is within one's power to punish or harm. The key word here is forgiveness. Grace gets us to a savable point, and mercy washes away our sins like the flood did for Noah.

The Ark

So faith and grace produced a pattern, and time and design produced a man. Thus, God called forth Noah out of the chaos of that age and instructed him to build the Ark, the pattern of his salvation:

> Make yourself an Ark of gopher wood; make rooms in the Ark, and cover it inside and outside with pitch. And this is how you shall make it: The length of the Ark shall be **three hundred** cubits, its width **fifty cubits**, and its height **thirty cubits**. You shall make a window for the Ark, and you shall finish it to a cubit from above; and set the door of the Ark in its side. You shall make it with **lower**, **second**, and **third** decks. (Genesis 6:14–16)

Now, I wish we had time and space here to explain the dimensions of the Ark and their link to Calvary because, as I said, hiding in among those dimensions is yet another pattern and another message. Unfortunately, we'll have to do that in the next chapter; and even then, I'm not sure we can fully exhaust the depth of its meanings and its numeric links to the construction of the universe; but we'll try. Lying beneath the surface of the Bible is a whole other allegorical world just waiting to be discovered like some lost city buried beneath the sands of time. In the next chapter, we will uncover some of their meanings; but for now, we will stick with the water and its symbolism.

So now that we have a little better understanding of how God patterns His allegories and orchestrates the lives of men, we can now begin to look at how He would use this water to further build His redemptive pattern. The day had finally come. It was time to enter the Ark and begin this long-awaited flood upon the earth and humanity. It was time to make it rain.

So then, the flood came:

> In the six hundredth year of Noah's life, in the second month, the seventeenth day of the month, on that day all the fountains of the great deep were broken up, and the windows of heaven were opened. And the rain was on the earth forty days and forty nights. Now the flood was on the earth forty days. The waters increased and lifted up the ark, and it rose high above the earth. The waters prevailed and greatly increased on the earth, and the ark moved about on the surface of the waters. And the waters prevailed exceedingly on the earth, and all the high hills under the whole heaven were covered. The waters prevailed fifteen cubits upward, and the mountains were covered. And all flesh died that moved on the earth: birds and cattle and beasts and every creeping thing that creeps on the earth, and every man. All in whose nostrils was the breath of the spirit of life, all that was on the dry land, died. So He destroyed all living things which were on the face of the ground: both man and cattle, creeping thing and bird of the air. They were destroyed from the earth. Only Noah and those who were

with him in the ark remained alive, and the waters prevailed on the earth one hundred and fifty days. (Genesis 7:11–12, 17–24)

So let the clouds fill with thunderous applause . . . and let lighting be the veins that fill the sky with all that they can drop . . . when it's time to make a change . . . make it rain... make it rain down Lord, make it rain. (Foy Vance)

Change

Change was the primary lesson here, and water would be used like a cocoon to create that change in either the course of Biblical events or someone's life. The flood was just the first in what would be a long line of examples, subtly revealing their true purpose with each passing shadow as they moved ever closer to the actual event of Calvary. Furthermore, this would become the founding principle that would one day lead us to not only the burial of the Christ but also His resurrection via a process I call the tomb and the womb.

Now, this concept of change through the use of water is nothing new; in fact, there were many ancient cultures that practiced various forms of water rituals, all with the intent to affect a change. If you track back through history, you'll find that many of the world's religions had seen water as both a literal and symbolic source of change. From the ancient Egyptian to the modern-day Christians, it seems that there has always been a universal undertone of purification and transformation surrounding the element. That's because water is the lifeblood of the entire planet, and it has long been seen by those ancient cultures as the conveyer between both the physical and the spiritual worlds. It is the universal conduit that lubricates the transition from the physical plane of life to the spiritual because water is the giver of life itself.

The Encyclopedia Britannica described water's spiritual implications like this:

The association between water and immortality is reflected in the myths of many cultures, myths that often center on a god-hero who sails away from his people in death with the promise to return again. The bodies of chiefs and heroes, therefore, have often been set adrift on rivers and oceans in death ships.

This is why many of the ancients, from the Vikings to the Hindus, preferred to bury their dead in it so often; even the ancient Greeks believed that they had to cross over the river Acheron to gain entrance into the underworld. This message is still transmitted to us today. How often have we in religious circles heard about crossing over the Jordan River when we die to enter the Promised Land? It seems that mankind cannot escape water's transitory powers. The ancients knew and fully understood the value of water and its connections between the worlds. And their symbolic concept of water was very much like the concept of the gods mingling their blood with the clay of the earth to form man. I believe they understood that blood provided the information and water provided the life.

Perhaps what we should be asking ourselves is what did our forefathers know about water that we don't? I mean, what was it about water that provoked so many to believe in it in such a way? Was it this great flood that they all drew upon for their spiritual information? Do you realize that there are over 500 ancient civilizations that have a flood story? It seems that water has always had a mystical hold on humanity's thoughts. It has only been in recent times that we as a modern society have devoiced ourselves from the symbolism that water carries. Why? Because the modern man views these ancient practices as primitive and superstitious, thus justifiably ignoring its symbolic importance and breaking off the pursuit of its meaning for fear of being viewed as religiously backward, never considering that it was still important to God. It's as if we have dismissed its former relevance to mankind's religious Dark Ages; chalk it up to ignorance right? Wrong, at least Biblically speaking; the symbolic power of water and its ability to create a change cannot be overlooked here, especially when it appears that there is a clear obsession with water by God.

So as cataclysmic as this flood was, from this point on, water would be used by God to create a change in the course of events or someone's life because its paramount objective was to act as the symbolic mercy of God. From the beginning, water was intended to be a part of the structure, the grand design. So like any good architect, God had already factored the loss of life into the design long before He ever broke ground. Why is the story of the flood and H_2O so complex? Because God had to transmit, or compress, so much information into one event that it nearly overwhelms the human senses. Not only was He installing physical information into the event, but also He was pushing into those symbolically spiritual realms. You understand that water, at least in the eyes of God, is the one element on the entire planet that possesses the unique ability in its natural liquid state to mimic not only the tomb of Christ but also the womb of God's creation. Now, I know at first you might be thinking, "How does this flood represent two symbolic types at the same time?" Well, actually it doesn't; it represents three, but as you will soon see, they are nearly identical in their intent.

How could all of that symbolism be hiding in one event? Well, first, we need to understand that this flood, and, more importantly, the water, is what gave God the unique ability and the best odds of displaying that future burial of Christ through the limited means of symbolism. There is nothing one could symbolically use to cover a living person and create a tomblike environment quite like water because it can very easily and without modification act as a tomb to cover someone. Remember that if He is never buried, then there is no resurrection; and that's why water was the perfect choice to symbolize and shadow the tomb of Christ; not only would it be through symbolic cleansing of the planet, purging it from the pollution of sin, as the grave did for Christ, but also it would be the perfect symbol of a tomb in its ability to completely cover without doing harm to the participants acting in that symbolic role.

With water, God did not have to actually kill and bury the person that was acting in the role of the Christ. He simply staged the allegory to do just that. And so therein lies one of the three reasons why God would use water to deliver His message—It easily becomes a symbolic grave in the way it can envelop the person or the event, thus making it the perfect symbolic element to connect us to the burial of Christ. The first reason, as mentioned before, was that it represented the mercy of God; and yet this is only a fraction of water's full biblical meaning.

Womb and the Tomb

The final symbolic purpose of the water was to replicate a womb. Now the catch is how does it go from being a tomb in the beginning of the allegory to becoming a womb by the end? Especially when the two places we're speaking of are about as completely opposite as two things can be. That's like saying black is white and white is black; the tomb and the womb are literally two worlds apart. One represents life and the other death, one a beginning and the other and ending—So how can that be? What was the purpose?

The first thing we need to understand about this whole process is that the womb and the tomb are both one and the same; they serve the same purpose because they are both used as a conveyance from one phase of life to the other. We all understand that the womb of our mothers brought us into our physical lives, holding us or encapsulating us in its amniotic fluid, which is about 90% water, until it was time to deliver us into our physical lives, thus completing the transfer from our protected life to one in the open. Whereas, upon our deaths, we are placed in a tomb or grave, generally speaking; and that place that is supposed to be of no return in reality becomes just another phase of our lives. The grave is serving the same purpose as our mother's wombs, just without the water, holding both body and soul in its womb like encapsulation, carrying its burdens like our mothers, waiting for the return of the Christ, waiting for the term of humanity to end so that it can deliver its souls into the afterlife.

The Apostle Paul brings to light this very core principle when he wrote:

> But I do not want you to be ignorant, brethren, concerning those who have fallen asleep (those who have died), lest you sorrow as others who have no hope. For **if we believe that Jesus died and rose again**, (there's your legal notice) even so God will bring with Him those who sleep in Jesus. For this we say to you by the word of the Lord, that we who are alive and remain until the coming of the Lord will by no means **precede those who are asleep**. For the Lord Himself will descend from heaven with a shout, with the voice of an archangel, and with the trumpet of God. **And the dead in Christ will rise first**. Then we who are alive and remain shall be caught up together with them in the clouds to meet the Lord in the air. (1 Thessalonians 4:13–17)

What Paul was saying here was that if Christ died and rose again, then so will we because the tomb or the grave is simply a womb that delivers us into our next and final phase of life. Looking to the Book of Acts, we find that Peter preached this very concept when he said:

> Men of Israel, hear these words: Jesus of Nazareth, a Man attested by God to you by miracles, wonders, and signs which God did through Him in your midst, as you yourselves also know. Him, being delivered by the determined purpose and foreknowledge of God, you have taken by lawless hands, have crucified, and put to death; whom God raised up, having **loosed the pains of death**, because it was not possible that He should be held by it. (Acts 2:22–24)

That word "pains" in the Greek literally means "birth pains," implying that God literally gave birth to Christ's body via death's womb, thus completing the transmission of the concept of the tomb not being the final stop. And so, in the case of our flood allegory here, we can clearly see how water can very easily and without modification also replicate a womb, especially seeing that a real womb is again about 90% water. But the overall message here was in the symbolic sequence of events, where we see that Noah went into that Ark, like Christ went into that tomb, a dead man soon to be buried by this coming flood, only to be resurrected some time later when he came out of the Ark into a new life and a new world.

So you see, water was used to transmit the very shadowy message that one day, the Christ would die and be buried and that He would rise again from a different kind of womb and become a new creation. God saw everything as a rebirthing process, an endless cycle for mankind to go from one womb to the next womb, from the physical womb of our mothers to the symbolic womb of the water, birthing those He had chosen into their spiritual journey with Him, and finally to the tomb, which became just another womb in the circle of life. Why in such a fashion? Because His Christ would go through the same process in the endeavor to save the creation, transitioning from life to death, to life again, and thus becoming what the Bibles calls "the first born of all the dead."

As we turn again to the Apostle Paul who delivers yet another profound concept to us when he wrote:

> He (Jesus) is the image of the invisible God, **the firstborn over all creation** (meaning Revelation 13:9). For by Him all things were created that are in heaven and that are on earth, visible and invisible, whether thrones or dominions or principalities or powers. All things were created through Him and for Him. And **He is before all things**, and in Him all things consist. And He is the head of the body, the church, who is the beginning, **the firstborn from the dead, that in all things He may have the preeminence**. (Colossians 1:15–18)

Simply put, everything was created with Christ in mind because He would be the one to redeem the creation. And so if He was to be first in all things, the first in creation as the lamb slain before the foundation of the world and the firstborn Son of God through the womb of Mary, then He would also have to be the firstborn of the dead through the tomb, which is the true womb of God that births all of humanity into that spiritual realm; therefore He would also need to be the first to ascend into heaven. All so that He could have the preeminence or be the first in all things. This is why God created this whole concept of the womb and the tomb and linked them both together with water; it represented both so easily.

Now, I know that death and life coming from the same place seems counterintuitive, but the reality here is that God doesn't see it that way. He sees the end from the beginning; He sees beyond the physical. He sent His only Son to the cross because He understood the separation between the two. He knew that one day, the Son would return to Him in that eternal spirit form. So what was He really losing? Nothing, I assure you, but it is what He would gain through that death; that was the paramount objective here. Because through that death, burial, and ultimate resurrection, God would not only show openly that He broke the curse of death that Adam had ushered in so long ago but also gain the redemption of the creation that had fallen away in that event. Christ would be the first to lead the way from the tomb and prove to us that it is not final, but rather just another part of the birthing process that is the cycle of God's creation. He was not going to put the creation through what He Himself would not go through first. As we know, if someone leads the way, then the rest will follow without fear. God weighed the cost of the flood, just as He would one day weigh the cost of Calvary, and decided that it was good that one, namely, Noah, should die a symbolic death for the many, just as the Christ would offer Himself up willingly to the tomb for the creation. Noah willingly offered himself up to this symbolic death for the sake of rebirthing humanity, just as the Christ would offer Himself up to the cross for the sake of saving humanity when He said, "Father, if you are willing, take this cup from me; yet not my will, but yours be done" (Luke 22:42).

The Allegory

So we see that the need for redemption overrode the value of physical life in both cases; there was a greater need here to save the souls of man, rather than the lives of man; and before you go calling God a monster, remember that Christ went back and preached to those souls and led them all out of that captivity and into heaven. And again, we see that there is more to this story than formerly thought. Because, this allegory was trying to accomplish what the grave of Christ would do in one simple step. But then again, the sheer complexity of this story is a display of the power behind the burial of the Christ. It is plain to see that this could not be defined or surmised in just a few simple terms; the burial and resurrection was a highly complex allegorical design that would take thousands of years and many examples to fully transmit its message. But by condensing three meanings into one allegorical step, God was sure to keep its simplicity shrouded in mystery.

Not only would the flood parallel Calvary in the death, burial, and resurrection, but also the life of Noah was designed to mirror that of the Christ. They were both born of a woman into postevent worlds; for Noah, it was a post-Garden world; and for Christ, it was a postflood world. They were also both seen as preachers of righteousness, where each warned the world of the coming judgments of God. Moreover, we see that each would die in a flood. For Noah, it was a symbolic death, being covered by the waves of judgment; but, for the Christ, it was a literal death, dying under the flood of humanity's sins, much in the same way the inhabitants of that early world were buried beneath the waves for their sins. And upon His resurrection, He would leave those sins behind in the grave like Noah left the sins of that former world. Furthermore, in the case of His rebirth or resurrection, instead of rising into a new world, it would be into a new phase of life, a true "born again" one, free of the chains of mortality and the fear of death. We also see that they both shared in the experience of a tomb—Noah's being the Ark made of wood and Christ's tomb being made of stone.

And interestingly enough, we find that the very thing that brought death in each account also brought life, ushering each one into a true "born again" event, thus proving that the tomb is not the final stop for humanity, but merely another womb that holds both body and soul for a term, waiting to deliver its contents to their final reward.

So, now we know that this water becomes a symbolic tomb, which then becomes a womb for all those acting in the role. We also know that they are changed symbolically from their physical state to a spiritual one, all to simulate what would happen to the Christ in His transition from a flesh-bound man to a spiritual being through His burial and resurrection. We also know now that the water is used as a catalyst by God to convert one from a state of death when they enter the water to a state of life or resurrection when they leave the water. What we are not sure of is where the change actually takes place in the allegory. And in truth, that's the question that has eluded us for quite some time. What's really happening back there in the ether of spiritualism in all of those stories? Where is that mystical point of change of the participants? If I had to take a guess, it would be at the point where the submersion ceased and the resurrection from the water began. But this is why God would choose water as the symbolic bonding element between both the womb and the tomb, serving as both simultaneously. Water gave God that unique ability to accomplish both a shadow of the death and the rebirth all wrapped into one element. Water was the only thing that would work to serve as both, and so this is the third and final reason why God used water.

So as you can see, water has been the most problematic of all explanations for the believer, because for so long we could not definitively say that this allegorical action means "this or that," or does "this or that," because we could not assign a definite value to it until the pattern was discovered. The depth and complexity of the allegories are often too difficult to understand when one is transmitting spiritual intent through the use of physical means. All too often, we are left unsure of our discoveries, unless you find enough examples to build a definitive answer where you remove any doubt about what the meaning truly is.

The Riddle of Water

So in closing, let me show you what I mean by complex by giving you what I call the riddle of water. As we know, water, or H_2O as it is known in its molecular structure, is composed of two elements, existing in three parts—two parts hydrogen and one part oxygen. Interestingly enough, the number three just so happens to be the symbolic biblical number for birth and rebirth, which is accomplished through the use of water. Furthermore, the earth just so happens to be the third planet from the sun, which is covered with, you guessed it, water. Again, this is the only known planet to possess it in its liquid state; and, oddly enough, the only planet in our perceivable universe that God chose to create His womb for life. Moreover, water is the only known element that can exist in three different states, even at the same time, being solids, liquids, and gas. And to top it all off, water in its biblical context represents three symbolic types—the tomb, the womb and the mercy of God.

As you can see, the number three is remarkable, tied to not only water but also our planet and our faith. So what do you think the odds are that all these things would share in the same numeric relationship? Pretty high, I'm sure. So then, the riddle is this: Did God create water with all these things in mind, and did He engineer all these things to be related so that one day we could see just how much He is involved in the creation business? Furthermore, did He place the earth in that third position from the sun, which is a symbol of Himself, to transmit that same message of birth and rebirth to us? All those questions I can't answer; but if I could speculate, then yes, He absolutely did, especially seeing how patterned the universe and the Bible both are.

But do you see what I mean by complicated? The deeper one digs, the more complex the questions become, until you reach a point that the questions cannot be answered. You simply have to walk away and hope that one day, you can. It was always God's intent to use the waters of the earth as the womb of His creation. From the moment He saw it and knew its placement in the universe, He intended to use those waters as the amniotic fluids of a womb, holding all of creation within its information and mineral-rich waters until it was time to call forth the living creatures upon the planet.

The whole process of creation was literally a womb inside of a womb, a pattern inside of a pattern, meaning that not only was the Ark telling a story of Calvary, but also Noah's life; and if you zoom out even further, you'll see that the earth followed the same process. We see the earth formed in the womb of creation and brought to life in the beginning, only to die and be buried beneath the waves of the flood; and then, we see her resurrected when the flood subsided. Life, death and life again, death, burial, and resurrection—It is the driving pattern of the entire Bible. God is the master of placing the complex ideal inside a simple meaning. It was His display of creative ability to use a womb to bring forth life and a tomb as well. The Bible and its complex mysteries were intentional, hidden in simple designs because God knew that, given enough time, man and his ways would pervert them and twist them to suit their needs.

So this flood was simply the first in what would be a long line of types and shadows using water. It all had to start somewhere, right? Just like the process of creating life, the pattern starts simply, with the combining of information from the father and the mother; but then, the cells begin to divide faster and faster; and this new creation becomes more and more complex. It begins to form limbs and organs until it reaches a stage where it is fully developed. And so the pattern works much in the same way. It starts out simple, forming in the deep obscure shadows of meaning; but soon, it divides and grows with each event, becoming more and more complex until the pattern is fully developed and birth is imminent. This is why Paul wrote, "But when the fullness of the time had come, God sent forth His Son, born of a woman, born under the law, to redeem those who were under the law, that we might receive the adoption as sons" (Galatians 4:4–5).

When the pattern was fully developed, it was time to deliver the Christ, the true pattern, that we might become the sons of God. Who knew that there was that much to water? I could go on, but there is little room and time for such things, perhaps in the future?

Ashes . . . take me back to Earth . . . **water** . . . quench my human thirst. (Ocean Lab)

Then I will sprinkle clean **water** upon you, and you will be clean: from all your filthiness, and from all your idols, I will cleanse you. (Ezekiel 36:25)

CHAPTER 5

❦

The Allegory of the Ark

1.66666667

> It is shocking to find out how many people do
> not believe they can learn, and how many more
> believe learning is difficult. (Dune)

Learning, that's all we're doing here is learning; but like the quote, many people think learning is hard. In reality, though, once one learns to focus their minds on the task at hand, then, over time, it becomes easier. As the Taoists say, "Be the master of your mind; don't let your mind be your master." In a broader scope, what they mean is that people have the tendency to lose control of their thoughts by focusing on the trivial things in life, thus derailing themselves in the process of learning. It is a training process that, like anything, takes time to acquire.

That is unless you can find a topic that will hold someone's attention, and for many, the topic of God and the Bible is high on that list. So, as promised in the last chapter, we will now touch on the dimensions of the Ark and their meaning. And again, like the other examples, this was always intended to be a foundational pattern that would one day take us all the way to Calvary. So what I want to do here is teach you not only what the numbers mean on the surface but also the process of equating those numbers into that allegorical message. It's that whole "teach a man how to fish" idea. If you learn this, you learn it for life; and besides, it will help to fill in the blanks to some of our biblical questions concerning numbers and dimensions. I hope you are ready because you are about to wake up to a whole new world.

Now, since I've been in church, I have never really understood the Bible's numbers, but neither has anyone else that I have known. Oh sure, the surface meanings are quite obvious, like those seven days of creation; but, to be honest, what most people know about them is what they have read. There has been no new exploration in the area because they feel like it has all been done. Yet there is still uncharted numeric territory out there, most of which lies in the dimensions of those things constructed. And it is not the fact that no one else has ever crunched the numbers on such things; it is just that no one has been able to decipher their meanings. And that is because we did not have a guideline on how to compute them. We did not have a clear path that said what our outcomes actually meant, and without that, it was much more difficult to establish allegorical intent. Again, we are dealing with pure symbolism. Besides that, I believe most people are intimidated by numbers; they have a way of doing that.

So I guess the first question should be "Are numbers really important to God?" Well apparently so because if you have ever read the Bible, you have probably noticed that throughout its entire course, it is full of numbers and dimensions. From Genesis to Revelation, numbers play a huge role in the construction and the transmission of its ideas. We see their use in everything from the seven days of creation right down to the 1260 days the two witnesses would prophesy in Revelation. So to say that numbers are everywhere in the Bible is kind of an understatement. They are more than just present; they are literally woven into the entire fabric, and their meanings, though sometimes elusive, are not arbitrary. They obviously meant something to God, but the question is what? And just because we don't know, or because we are not willing to invest the time into their solution, does not mean that we can simply cast them aside. To do so is to overlook one of the Bible's greatest treasures. God put them there for a reason. So who are we to decide their relevance? Anyone who understands the relevance of numbers will not deny the fact that the Bible's numbers are important. Look at what astrophysicist Mario Livio had to say about the Bible's numbers:

> Numbers were fundamental realities, drawing symbolic meanings from the relation between the heavens and human activates. Furthermore, essentially no number that was ever mentioned in the holy writings was ever treated as irrelevant. (The Golden Ratio)

I think for the most part, we can all agree that the Bible's numbers matter; but again, for most of us, the problem hasn't been in believing that they mean something. The problem has been that it is often difficult to find those underlying meanings; but there is a reason for that. If God had just spelled them all out on the surface, then surely by now, man would have found a way to twist them to his intent. And I'm not talking about finding your social security number or your phone number in those underlying meanings. That's lunacy and only proves that coincidences happen. I'm not looking for that, and neither should you. I'm looking to further my understanding of the Bible and God's intentions for man. But then that brings us back to the same question: How does one know what is truth, especially with numbers?

Simple—with patterns. They produce predictability, which proves that it's not a coincidence. Sure if something happens once or twice, that's a coincidence. But if it happens time and time again, then no—that's a pattern—which proves that something is deliberate; Biblical patterns prove the existence of a designer. You realize that one simply does not stumble haphazardly into repeated patterns, especially allegorical and numerical ones; again, that proves design. And I can't even begin to imagine what the odds are on having consistent patterns in a book that has sixty-six subbooks, written by multiple writers and spanning some several thousand years. The conspiracy of genius would itself be on a divine level.

But then that leads us to another question: Why are there patterns in the numbers? God uses numbers as yet another level of that veiled speech we touched on earlier. Just as He uses the allegories to reveal the subtle truths of the Bible, He also uses numbers in the same manner; they are just another way of transmitting a message. The numbers themselves are layered much in the same way the stories are: There is one message being transmitted on the surface; and if you dig, you'll find that there is an underlying allegorical message unfolding at the same time, again, a perfect example of the macro- and the microcosm.

The Designer

Now, I'm sure you're thinking, why would God do that? Why would He hide His message in such a complicated way? He did it because math is the universal language; and you will find that, at His core, God is a mathematician. He loves numbers, and He loves using them in the context of His messages because it is a display of His creative knowledge and power. And if man discovers their meanings, then great; he has proven himself worthy of studying; and if he doesn't get it, then no worries, because it really doesn't change the outcome of the overall message, as the allegories took care of that. The numbers are simply, as the Cajuns say, "lagniappe," a little extra gift. Again, they are there for the diligent; and when you discover them, they become yet another proof that this was all by design, a design far beyond the possibilities and scope of any human. As Michael Drosnin said in his book the *Bible Code II*:

> The greatest scientist who ever lived, the man who single-handedly invented modern science, Sir Isaac Newton, was certain that not only the Bible, but the entire universe, was a "cryptogram set by the Almighty," a puzzle that God made, and that we were meant to solve.

If you don't think that's true, then consider the construction of our universe for just a minute. Under close examination, you will find that everything in it is ordered by mathematical principles and patterns. Yes, everything is obedient to math. Let's consider the simple-looking, yet complex logarithmic spiral that's in figure 1. This derives its name from the way in which its radius grows as you move around the curve, which naturally produces self-symmetry, meaning it does not alter its shape as its size increases. Now, the spiral maintains this perfect distance between its inner coils as it grows from the center by specifically turning on equal angles as it increases the distance from the center by equal ratios, thus displaying its highly complex nature and design. This allows for an infinite spiral because if you were to enlarge the coils that are invisible to the eye, they would fit precisely on the larger spiral.

Why does this spiral matter in our universe of equations? It can be found in nearly every aspect of cosmic and organic life. From spiral-wound galaxies and black holes to flowers and sea animals here on earth, its universal influence is only matched by Pi, and it all speaks of a designer. Quoting again from Mario Livio on the subject, "Nature loves logarithmic spirals. From sunflowers, seashells, and whirlpools, to hurricanes and giant spiral galaxies, it seems nature chose this marvelous shape as its favorite ornament."

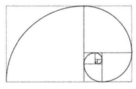

Figure 1

Remember that these things turn on equal angles and by equal ratios, which is impossible if they were just random acts of nature, right? We all know that order does not just spring out of randomness. So then we should be asking ourselves how this is possible. How can so many diverse things in the universe share in the same spiral pattern? Well, in a Darwinian world of random selection, they can't;

but in the real world of mathematics, we see that they share in the same design because the design itself implies that there is a designer. Mathematics is everywhere, like God Himself. They are both omnipresent, and mathematics alone should prove that there is a designer because there are rule and laws that govern their use and existence. But that's how a sunflower and our galaxy can share in the same mathematical principle; they were both designed by the same engineer. Look, if He didn't change the relationship between the creation of the earth and a woman's womb, then He surely would not have changed His design for a logarithmic spiral. Why choose this spiral? They are engineered in such a way as to optimize growth and to keep natural balance and proportion.

So I think it's safe to say that our creator is a mathematician. Mind you, that's just one example. There are mathematical relationships in everything organic—Entire books have been written on these very subjects. Just go get a book on Pi, or Phi, and you'll begin to see how everything is interconnected by mathematical principles. In fact, it's all so connected that it's downright spooky. It seems the harder I look, the more I find that everything in our universe is ordered. And that's because mathematics is not only the language of the universe but also the language of God. You realize that God can not only create with numbers but also speak with them, in fact just as easily as He can with words. It's nothing for God to display an allegorical meaning through numbers; it would be the same as expressing it in words because there is no difference to Him. It's just what He likes to do because by doing so, He displays His supreme intellect through numerical use, as Lord Kelvin once said, "When you cannot express it in numbers, your knowledge is of a meager and unsatisfactory kind."

God has never had a problem expressing His message through numbers because there is no intellectual boundary; the only problem in explaining His numbers has come from us and our intellectual boundaries. Look, if computers can talk in 1s and 0s, and those are inventions of man, then how much more should God be able to? After all, He is mathematics in its grandest sense and ideas, and He is the creator of all such designs. Moreover, if we cannot express His message to mankind through the numbers He left us, then that really places our knowledge of His word as unsatisfactory. So yes, numbers are important to God and the transmission of His message, and as we go deeper into this, you'll see just what I mean, Alice.

Now, for anyone who has ever read the Bible and the story of Noah's Ark, you have probably wondered like the rest of us why was the Ark built on those dimensions? Surely, there was a reason for that; they can't be there just to be there, right? Right, but again, the long-standing problem has always been how to find that meaning, and what method do we use to equate those numbers beyond the surface meaning into something we can all understand? Because there really was a reason why God was so specific in His designs; you realize He could have just said, "Build an ark big enough to hold all the animals"; but then, the odds of building an Ark that reflected an accurate picture of Calvary would be about as accurate as random selection. Remember that it's all about that day; everything was built on that concept, and knowing that helps us look for the answer.

Ratios

So what is the key to unlocking the numerical door of the Bible? Well, the answer is really quite simple; the key is ratios. What's a ratio? Well, a ratio is a comparison of two or more quantities that are related. In mathematics, a ratio is a relationship between two numbers indicating how many times the first number contains the second. For example, if a bowl of fruit contains eight oranges and six lemons, then the ratio of oranges to lemons is eight to six (i.e., 8:6), which is equivalent to the ratio 4:3 if reduced to it to its lowest common denominator. Thus, a ratio can also be a fraction as opposed to a whole number, like ⅔. Furthermore, the numbers compared in a ratio can also be in any quantities of a comparable kind, such as objects, persons, or dimensions, as in the case of our Ark, which was in cubits, 300 length x 50 width x 30 height. You'll often see ratios written in forms such as "a to b" or "a:b." As for the Ark, we could express it like "a to b to c" or "300:50:30"; and sometimes, ratios can be expressed arithmetically as a quotient of the two, which is what we are going to ultimately do with the Ark and numerous biblical dimensions. What's a quotient? It is the result of division. For example, when dividing 6 by 2, the quotient is 3. Quotient simply means "how many times."

Ratios are the building blocks of the entire universe. Everywhere you look, from our solar system and the relationship between planets and the sun to planets and their moons, you will find ratios and their by-products. Take the earth and its moon, for example. Their rotation is set on a 1:1 ratio; that is why you will never see one inch more or less of the moon because it is perfectly synced with the earth in its rotation. And the more you look, the more you find ratios and their by-product. Even on the earth, ratios play a huge role by producing symmetry in nearly every living organism and for that matter even nonliving organic objects.

For example, animals have either bilateral or mirror symmetry, meaning that an object or figure that is indistinguishable from its transformed image is called mirror symmetric. You can even find symmetry in the leaves of plants and some flowers, like orchids. Moreover, plants often have radial or rotational symmetry, as do many flowers and some groups of animals such as sea anemones, which are all based on the logarithmic spiral. Even the lowly sea animals such as starfish and sea urchins have a mathematical fivefold symmetry, which when measured produces ratios that will again produce that same logarithmic spiral. Mathematical symmetry can even be found among nonliving things, such as crystals and snowflakes, which have a sixfold symmetry, where each flake is unique in its structure. And the list doesn't stop there; mathematical symmetry can be found in almost everything, from waterdrops splashing into larger bodies of water to the rings around planets, all of which are by-products of ratios.

Now, I said all of that to say this—There are two quotient or numeric by-products of ratios that are pervasive in our universe that touch on nearly everything; in fact, it's quite difficult to find anything that is organic that does not produce one of the two, if not both, numeric expressions. The two numbers I'm talking about are known in the mathematical world as Pi π and Phi Φ, respectively, 3.14159 . . . and 1.61803399 . . ., in their numeric expressions.

And so it is from that simple combination of a ratio that two of the most complex irrational numbers known to man are produced. Irrational means that it can't be expressed as a fraction of two whole numbers, and its decimal representation is an infinite string of digits with no repeating pattern that goes on forever. They are the by-product of combining numbers that share a common object. For example, Pi is achieved by creating a ratio between a circle's circumference (C) and its diameter (D), $\frac{C}{D} = \pi$, or it can be expressed by its more commonly known equation, $A = \pi r^2$. Now, I probably don't have to tell you about all the things that are naturally round in our universe to convince you that Pi is ubiquitous; it is quite literally universal, and understanding it and its numeric outcome has been one of mankind's crowning mathematical achievements. Pi is a clear by-product of creation, a creation that began with ratios.

As for Phi, its outcome is a little more complex because it creates what is known as the "golden ratio." In mathematics, two quantities are in what is known as the golden ratio if their ratio is the same as the ratio of their sum to the larger of the two quantities. Simply put, if you divide a:b and the outcome is 1.618 . . ., then you should be able to add a:b, take that total, and divide it against the larger quantity of a:b and get the same outcome of 1.618 . . . If so, then it is considered golden, such as is found in figure 2.

$$\frac{a+b}{a} = \frac{a}{b} = \varphi.$$

Figure 2

So remember that logarithmic spiral that has all those things connected to its design? Well, it is a by-product of ratios that produce the numeric oddity of Phi, or 1.61803399 . . . This mathematical anomaly can also be found throughout numerous geometric shapes, like pentagrams and pentagons; and there is even a Golden triangle, which can be used to also create a logarithmic spiral, simply because the intersecting lines are all at the same golden point. Even fruit bears these shapes and ratios; just cut an apple in half along the girth of it, and what you find on the inside is a perfect pentagram. It simply amazes me just how prevalent these shapes are in nature, once again proving that things in the universe are not just happenchance, but divinely ordered. And believe it or not, there is a rational reason for using irrational numbers in creation.

Let's take Pi, for example, but Phi works much in the same way on this process. So, in nature, we know that plant stalks are, of course, round; and we all know that Pi is used to equate the circumference of anything round, right? But, what we find from our equation is that it is only an approximation of the circumference of the circle. Why? Because Pi is infinite—The numbers go on forever. Now, I'm sure you're thinking, "But if I measure the circumference with a tape I will have a stopping point, a fixed measurement," right? Well no, and that's simply because if you magnified the location of your stopping point on the circumference, you would see that it is no longer at that point, but it is a little shorter; and the more you magnify the stalk, the further away you original point becomes. This is known as the study of the infinite, and it has literally driven several men to the point of madness because they have tried to find the end of something that is infinite. Now, here's the rationale behind using such a number in creation: When that plant stalk begins to sprout leaves along its circumference, Pi and its irrational never-ending numbers insure that the plant will never put a leaf in the exact location as one before it. By design, you will never have one leaf exactly over another because of Pi's irrational numbering sequence. Why does that matter? It insures optimal light and water absorption for the plant, thus the rational use of irrational numbers in creation.

And that is my point of this whole lesson: Everything is ordered essentially by ratios. All of creation is participating in a mathematical symphony right before us in what Joseph Schillinger called unconscious art; organic life is simply the art of creation where the ratios lend to the symmetry and balance of all things. Ratios and their by-products are at the heart of creation; they are among its simplest forms, like addition and subtraction; yet they speak volumes in everything we see. They are everywhere, like God, so it stands to reason that if God built creation on ratios and their quotient, then He would have also used ratios in the creation of His book, right? And so He did as you will soon see.

Now, we are not going to do any crazy math here, just plain and simple as it should be, because understanding God should never be difficult. God wanted to make finding His answers simple enough that we could all do it; we just needed to know the process. Remember that He never left us an instruction manual on how all this works; that was left up to us to figure out. So understanding that the process is the key that unlocks the door, which begins with setting up ratios from our given quantities and those ratios, in turn, will give us our numeric answers. Mind you, they don't explain what the numbers mean; they only unlock them. To understand that, you'll have to have a basic knowledge of what each number means. Again, I could just tell you that 2+2=4. But if I don't teach you how to do it for yourself, then how does that help you? It still leaves you in the dark, but if you learn how to equate truth, then we can all step into the light.

The Base Numbers

So on the biblical surface, each number represents or means something different and of course combinations of numbers as well. For instance, the number one is considered the generator of all numbers and is the representation of the point in geometry, which makes it the generator of all dimensions as well and therefore the perfect representation of God. He is the progenitor of all things, the beginning of all dimensions. He is the first of everything and the beginning of reason, not to mention it is how He describes Himself, "Hear, O Israel: The Lord our God is **one** Lord" (Deuteronomy 6:4).

Now, the number two in biblical terms is considered to be the number of separation or division because God divided or separated the waters from the waters on the second day. There were two cherubs built into the lid of the Ark of the Covenant, symbolically demonstrating that this is where God would separate Israel from their sins year after year. There were also two angels found in the tomb of the

Christ after His resurrection to symbolize the same meaning as the Ark—that humanity had finally been separated from their sins. Even among the ancient Greeks, two (2) was considered to be the number of opinion and division. Interesting side note for the number two— It is the smallest and the first prime number in our base 10 series, as well as being the only even prime number, and the square root of two produces an irrational number much like those found in our creation process.

As for the number three, it is symbolic of birth and rebirth and of course water. It was on the third day that God birthed the dry land from the waters. There were also three steps to the rebirth of the Christ—death, burial, and resurrection—which are the very steps that govern the entire pattern of Calvary. And it is through that three-step process that God decided to use those various symbolic means, or quantities, that represented the pattern through the use of (1) blood, (2) water, and (3) the miraculous or by the symbolic colors of (1) red, (2) blue, and (3) purple, of which we will get to later. The Pythagoreans considered the number three to be the first real number because it had a "beginning," a "middle," and an "end," unlike the number two, which has no middle. Interestingly enough, three depicts the biblical cycle of life, death and rebirth, as mentioned. In step one, we are born; then in step two, we die; and in step three, we are resurrected from the grave, born again—a beginning, middle, and an end. All things in the Bible's rebirthing process always acted out in sets of three, no matter what the symbolic quantities were.

The number four represents light and life, which we now know are one in the same, as it was on the fourth day that God created the sun, the moon, and the stars. Once they were in place, life could then begin on the planet, not only because of the sunlight but also because of the gravity that the sun would now lend to the earth and begin its solar orbit. This is where actual time began for the earth because days and nights could be marked off and the seasons were set into motion. Interestingly enough, John equated the same principles of light and life to the Christ when he wrote, "In Him (Christ) was life, and the life was the light of men. And the light shines in the darkness, and the darkness did not comprehend it" (John 1:4–5).

Furthermore, the cross in which the light of the world hung on has four sides to it—top, bottom, and the two sides, left and right. There are also four letters in the name of God: JHVH. And there were four rivers flowing out from Eden where all life began. They were the Pishon–Gihon–Tigris–Euphrates (Genesis 2:10–14). So four is the number of light and life.

The number five is the number of grace in the Bible because it was by His grace that He began to bring forth all the living creatures on the fifth day. There are also five books of God's Law that was a symbol of His grace imparted to man in the form of these books, (Genesis, Exodus, Leviticus, Numbers, and Deuteronomy) that are commonly referred to as the Pentateuch ("Penta" meaning five). Furthermore, the Ten Commandments contain two sets of five commandments. The first five commandments are related to our treatment and relationship with God, and the last five concern our relationship with others humans. The number five was also considered by the Pythagoreans to be the union of the first female number two, with the first male number three; and as such, it was considered the number of love and marriage. Interestingly enough, out of that union, life begins, just like on day five. It is also essential in the creating of Phi because there are five points in a pentagram and pentagon, which give us our infinite irrational number that is so inextricably linked to the designs of the Creator.

The number six is seen as the number of man because man was created on the sixth day. Furthermore, man was designed with six major parts of the human body—one head, one torso, two arms, and two legs. This is also a partial display of one of the most common numbers of the Bible, the number 12. This number 12 originally comes about because on the 6th day, God created man (6), 6+6=12. What I mean by that is that the divine spiritual Creator created the fleshly man on that day, thus not only symbolizing man's need for the creator but also displaying the connection between the two sides of man's existence, the spiritual and the physical. This is one of the reasons why the number 12 was used so frequently in the Bible. It is a representation of when God created His greatest creation: man.

The other reason was in the reverse fashion where we see that Adam (6) was created on the 6th day, again a symbol of the fleshly carnal side of creation that brought sin and death into the world. And on the other side of the equation, we see Christ (6), the perfect man, that symbolized the spiritual side of creation and who gave His life to remove the curse of sin and death. So, 6 carnal + 6 spiritual = 12.

The Apostle Paul points out this connection between the two men when he wrote:

> Therefore, as through one man's offense (Adam) judgment came to all men, resulting in condemnation, even so through one Man's righteous act (Christ) the free gift came to all men, resulting in justification of life. For as by one man's disobedience many were made sinners, so also by one Man's obedience many will be made righteous. (Romans 5:18–19)

So again, the number 12 is symbolic of the two men that changed the course of humanity, Adam and Christ, 6+6=12. You will see 12 used often in the Bible because it is symbolic of humanity's dual nature, the spirit of God and the flesh of man—a clear use of the macro- and the microcosm.

Now, I would like to dispel a little biblical myth here about the number six because it has often been called the number of man and imperfection. Why? Because a perfectly created man Adam (6) did something imperfect by sinning against God. Understand, though, that the actions of the man do not make the number itself imperfect. Man's actions have no bearing on the number's meaning or significance; the number is simply symbolic of the man. Remember that God does not create anything imperfect. One only has to look as far as the human body to see that it is perfect in its design, perfect in its balance, and perfect in its symmetry with its six parts. So how can the number six be a symbol of imperfection? The simple answer is it cannot.

To prove my point though, let's look at what some pretty credible people had to say about the number six and its importance:

> The number 6 is the first **perfect** number, as well as the number of creation. The adjective "perfect" was attached to numbers that are precisely equal to the sum of all the smaller numbers that divide into them, as 6 = 1+2+3. (Mario Livio, The Golden Ratio)

Furthermore, the Hellenistic Jewish philosopher Philo Judaeus of Alexandria suggested that "God created the world in 6 days because 6 was a **perfect** number." In addition, the same idea was elaborated upon by St. Augustine in his book *The City of God*, where he said, "Six is a number **perfect** in itself, and not because God created the world in six days; rather the contrary is true: God created the world in six days because this number is **perfect**, and it would remain **perfect**, even if the work of the six days did not exist."

So the number six is the number of man, the first perfect number. There is even a message for us in the sum of those smaller divisible numbers, 1+2+3, that is God (1) + will separate (2) + us from sin and give us new life (3) = through the perfect man, Christ (6), 1+2+3=6. Besides that little fact, there is a reason why I sought to remove the shadow that was over this number, as you'll soon see.

As for the number seven, it is the biblical number of completion, rest, and perfection. Again looking to creation, God completed the work of creation and rested on the seventh day. According to Rabbi Nachmanides, seven is also the number of the natural world. There are seven days in the week, seven notes on the musical scale, and seven directions (left, right, up, down, forward, back, and center). There are also seven colors in a rainbow and seven openings in the head. The number seven is used 735 times throughout the course of the Bible, which is divisible by the number seven 105 times, which of course if you divide 735/105, it goes right back to 7. All of these point to a completed and perfect creation. Moreover, the number seven is probably one of the most commonly written numbers in history because of its direct association with the Creator. As we move through the book, I will be sure to point out each example that the number seven is used so that you can see its symbolism in action. So that's the first seven numbers. Mind you, I would like to carry on with these base numbers, but I fear we would run out of room. Besides, I will address them throughout the book when we stumble upon them.

The Ark

Now, in the case of the Ark, we will touch on its numbers and their surface meanings very briefly. We will start with (300) because it was the first one given. It means "The Great, The Mighty God," and it also means "The Spirit of God." This meaning is derived from an ancient form of Jewish numerology known as Gematria which is an alphanumeric system of code/cipher that assigns numerical value to a word or phrase in the belief that words or phrases with identical numerical values bear some relation to each other or bear some relation to the number itself. Basically, each word has a number value, and each number has a word value. The Jews use this method to convert numbers and words into deeper scriptural meanings, much in the same way Ivan Panin did, thus converting our number 300 into its meaning.

For the number (50), we will be using the same method, which means "all or everything," in Gematria; and it is also the number of "jubilee or deliverance." It was in the 49th year going into the 50th year that the celebration of Jubilee occurred, and it lasted for one solid year. During that celebration, slaves and prisoners were set free, debts would be forgiven, and the mercies of God would be particularly manifested toward the people. It truly was a year of deliverance. It would also be on the 50th day after the Exodus that God would descend upon Mount Sinai and begin the process of delivering all of the law to Israel. Moreover, it would be on the 50th day after the death of Christ, the day of Pentecost, that God would for the first time give mankind everything He had intended for them by pouring out His Spirit upon humanity.

And finally the number (30) that is symbolic of "change" or a "life change" in the Bible; it is a sign of maturing of a person or a shadow. Many of the Bible's key figures experienced a complete change in their lives at this age. Joseph was 30 years old when he was released from prison and became second in command to the pharaoh. The priests also officially entered service at the age of 30. David became king when he was 30 years old, and Ezekiel was called by God as a prophet at age 30. Furthermore, John the Baptist was 30 years old when he came out from the wilderness to pave the way for the Messiah; and lastly, Jesus officially started His ministry at the age of 30 when He was baptized by John in the Jordan. All of these moments of maturing and change shadowed reflections of the coming Christ and the age when He would begin His ministry.

So the combined surface meaning of the Ark's numbers is, roughly, that "The Great, and The Mighty God" (300) will bring "deliverance" (50) from the flood to "All" who were in the Ark, and that it was to be a "Life Change" or "Maturing" (30) to all that were in the Ark. Overall, you get the meaning of what God was trying to transmit through the dimensions of the Ark. In essence, it was deliverance and a change for humanity.

Now that our basic numbers are out of the way, we can move on to creating our ratios out of the same numbers. What you're about to learn here is the principle that unlocks the meaning behind many of the Bible's numeric mysteries; in fact, it is essential to understanding how much God designed Calvary into everything. So once again, the surface numbers give us our ratios, the ratios give us our by-product, and the numeric by-product is the submessage that we will then decipher with our base seven numbers.

So, once more, the Ark's dimensions were 300L x 50W x 30H. Now, by taking any two numbers of the three that are in a given dimension like the Ark, we can begin to create our ratios and thus find our submessage. So let's start by taking the two smaller numbers and dividing them like so $\frac{50}{30} = 1.66666667$. Then, let's take the two larger numbers and divide them so that we get $\frac{300}{50} = 6$. So, on one scale, we get what is called a repeating decimal (.66666), which rounds up to a 7, somewhere out there in the infinite. And the other ratio gives us the whole number of 6. So, we are already beginning to see a bit of a pattern here; let's take it a little further to prove our equations.

Now, you can also reverse these same numbers, and they will produce an inverse of the original number, like so, $\frac{50}{300} = 0.16666667$, or $\frac{30}{50} = 0.6$ . . . So what does all of this mean? Well, it means that not only do we have our message in the normal equation, but also it is present in the inverse. For example, Phi or (Φ), which is 1.618 . . ., is how it appears in its proper function; this is known as an uppercase normal equation. But the inverse of the same numbers would look like this 0.618 . . ., and its symbols would appear in their lowercase to emphasize what they are phi or (φ). So what this ratio means is that frontward or backward, we get the same numbers and the same message, which is a good sign that we are on the right track.

Golden Ratio of Phi

So let's take this one step further by trying to apply the same principles that govern the formation of the golden ratio of Phi, which is displayed here in figure 3. This is done by first adding the numbers that we first used to create our ratios. Once that is done, we will then divide that number against the larger of the two we used to create the first ratio, thus creating another ratio to see if we get the same number. Let's work it out so you can see it in action. Now, we know that 50 divided by 30 gives us 1.66666667; and if we add the two like so (50+30), we get the sum of = (80). Now, we take that number (80) and create another ratio using the larger number of our original ratio, which was (50), so that the new ratio looks like this $\frac{80}{50} = 1.6$ or for the full equation would look like this $\frac{50+30}{50} = \frac{50}{30} = 1.6$. This is the very process in which one determines if a set of numbers is in what is called a golden relationship, meaning they produce the same outcome after one performs the function.

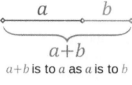

$a+b$ is to a as a is to b

Figure 3

So again, we see that we have the same outcome of 1s and 6s, which means that we now have a set of numbers that are in a very unique relationship with one another in their dimensions and their message and very close to the golden ratio of Phi itself. In fact, it's so close that it is only 48 hundredths off, which is hardly visible to the human eye at even a slight distance, especially if you are talking about something the size of the Ark. It is close, yes, but this number is quite unlike the golden ratio because it is a rational number instead of being irrational. Thus, it has a definite pattern to it, and it does not run on into infinity. So what's the meaning of this?

Well, remember the rational use of the irrational numbers? That applies only to the natural things that need that infinite possibility to exist, like our spiral-wound galaxies and plants; but the irrational cannot apply to a book that is based on rationale like the Bible now, can it? Especially seeing that irrational numbers are without patterns and infinite, how could you then place an explanation or give the meaning to a number that has no end? You can't! That whole process would be counterintuitive to what God was trying to teach us. Can you imagine trying to put an explanation to a number that never ends and has no pattern to it? Impossible!

So then what is the meaning of our number 1.66666667? Well, of course, it is first based on a definite pattern, as you can see by the 1s and 6s. Secondly, it is, as always, Christ-centered. So we will start the deciphering by using our base 7 numbers, seeing that there is nothing higher than a 7 in the sequence. Now, the first number in the sequence is of course (1), which is the number of God Himself. Not only is it the generator number of our equation, like God is the generator of everything, but also it is the only whole number in the entire sequence, which is a perfect representation of God, seeing that He is not divided.

Now, the second number will take some explaining because there are so many of them; in fact, I honestly really don't know how far out it keeps repeating itself. If we had just one (6), that would be easy to define because it is the number of man. But what we have here are multiple 6 that are running out to somewhere near infinity. Now, I personally like to stop them at seven places, (.6666666). Why seven? Well, not only is it the number of completion, but also it is because my calculator only runs them out to 14 places. That's just way too many 6s to be typing over and over. So we will stop at seven places.

So, again, we understand that 6 is the number and the symbol of man, and multiple sixes would imply multiple men, right? Now, if we don't know right offhand what this represents, then we must turn to the Bible to gain further understanding. There we will find that there are only three places in the entire Bible where multiple sixes appear, and they are all in the form of 666. Of course, our minds go directly to the book of Revelation and the infamous number of the Beast, which is synonymous with evil, but that surely can't mean our Ark is evil, now can it? No, it does not. Again, the man does not make the number evil; the number just identifies the man. Since 6 is the first perfect number, 666 would simply mean triple perfection.

Now, before I just come right out and tell you what it means, let me first explain what the other two uses of this number in the Bible means so you can better understand its outcome. So the first reference is to Solomon's annual allotment of gold, which was 666 talents: "The weight of gold that came to Solomon every year was six hundred and sixty-six talents of gold" (1 Kings 10:14). So did this imply that Solomon was evil?

No, of course not. In fact, the Bible calls him the wisest man that ever lived because he asked of God the wisdom to rule His people.

> Then God said to him: "Because you have asked this thing, and have not asked long life for your-self, nor have asked riches for yourself, nor have

asked the life of your enemies, but have asked for yourself understanding to discern justice, behold, I have done according to your words; see, I have given you a wise and understanding heart, so that there has not been **anyone like you** before you, nor shall **any like you** arise after you." (1 Kings 3:11–12)

And there's clue number one.

Another interesting fact about Solomon is that his throne had six steps leading up to it, symbolizing that he was still just a man in the eyes of God and of Israel, in a sense humbling himself before God. If it would have had seven steps, that would have put him in the position of God, and we see where that got Lucifer. Furthermore, on each of those six steps, there was a lion placed on either side, meaning that there were 12 lions flanking the steps to the throne, symbolizing the 12 tribes of Israel. The lion is the symbol of the tribe of Judah, and it is also a symbol of the Christ, who was also a descendant of David. This is why He is called "the lion of the tribe of Juda" in the Book of Revelation. It is all about symbolism.

Now, the next one comes in the Book of Ezra 2:13, which was a reference to the list of the men of Israel who were returning from Babylonian captivity. In this chapter, it gave a count of the sons of Adonikam, of which 666 returned. Now, not much can be found on the man, but the name means "my lord has risen up." I also found one reference that said that Adonikam was a noble under Artaxerxes, who was sent from Babylon to Jerusalem to rebuild the temple. The implication was that he was in some way connected to Hiram, the builder of Solomon's temple. I cannot confirm this because there is so little written about the man, and Nehemiah's account numbers them at 667. Not much to go on there, but certainly no reference to evil.

And of course last, but surely not the least, of this list is found in the Book of Revelation, "Here is wisdom. Let him who has understanding calculate the number of the beast, **for it is the number of a man**: His number is 666" (Revelation 13:18). And there's clue number two; but again, when most people hear or see this number, they think of evil. This is yet another misconception about the Bible that will of course take time to change because the number itself is not evil; it is merely pointing out an evil man. It is the identifier of the Beast. If the number were evil, then how could it be associated with Solomon or the remnant that came out of captivity to rebuild the temple? Did the number make Solomon evil? No, of course not. It's just that the numbers are merely transmitting a message, just like the throne of Solomon. That's why John wrote, "Let him who has **understanding** calculate the number of the beast."

What John meant was that understanding or knowledge is what is needed to look beyond the surface meaning of a mere number and into the true depths of this message. Starting at its surface meaning, John said that it was the number of a man, but the question is what kind of man? The explanation is simple, for you see, you and I are simply single 6s. We're nothing special, but the Beast is a triple 6, (666), meaning that this man that is to be the antichrist is going to be a man that is not only the personification of evil but also man multiplied, or man amplified, as if to suggest that there is 3 times more to this man than the average.

The Apostle Paul confirms his super human powers in the Book of Thessalonians:

> The coming of the lawless one is according to the working of Satan, with **all power**, **signs**, and **lying wonders**, and with **all unrighteous deception** among those who perish, because they did not receive the love of the truth, that they might be saved. (2 Thessalonians 2:9–10)

In short, he will be the most powerful man to set foot on the earth since Jesus; he will be that triple man, 666.

Going back to clue number one, this is the reason why Solomon's annual allotment of gold was 666 talents; it was a symbolic reference to his wisdom because he was, as the Bible says, the wisest man that ever lived. Therefore, he was given the extra 6s, and there is your final clue to our number. That's why the Ark possessed all those 6s;

it is the representation of a man, but again, what kind of man? Man amplified beyond all comparison, the Man Christ Jesus.

You see, the Ark with its ratio by-product of 1.66666667 is simple in its meaning. So simple in fact that it is easy to overlook, but when we put it through the lens of our new understanding, we get a clearer picture of what God was pointing to. Again in summation, the (1) symbolizes God in His singleness, undivided and unseparated, the oneness of the eternal Creator and designer of all things. He is the beginning of all measurements and all life, "In the beginning God created the heaven and the earth" (Genesis 1:1). And the seemingly endless 6s symbolize the perfect man, Christ Jesus. As for the (7), again, it is the number of completion, godly perfection and rest, that means that the 7 would be placed on the end to represent the man that would come as the complete and perfect cure for sin through His sacrifice and give us rest from ours.

That's why the Ark was able to save Noah and his family because it was the very symbol of God in Christ. That future union was built into the very design of the Ark that would save not only him symbolically but also the entire world literally. And that's why Noah could not deviate from those exact measurements. He would have mutated the pattern and messed up the blueprint for that future union of God and Christ and ultimately his salvation. And that's why the Apostle Paul made such statements as "to know that God (1) was in Christ (.66666667) reconciling the world unto Himself" (1 Corinthians 5:17). And in another place he wrote, "There is one (1) God, and one mediator between God and men, the **man** (.66666667) Christ Jesus" (1 Timothy 2:5).

And yet again, "And without controversy great is the mystery of godliness: God (1) was manifested in the flesh (.66666667), Justified in the Spirit, Seen by angels, preached among the Gentiles, believed on in the world, received up in glory" (1 Timothy 3:16). As you can see, that's our formula; the Ark was simply a symbol of what was to come, God in Christ, the complete and perfect union of God and man, (1) +(.66666667), thus completing the intended blueprint of the coming Christ and fulfilling the pattern of the Ark.

And it seems that he passed that knowledge along to Luke as well, seeing that he wrote of the same union after the baptism of Christ in the Jordan River, "and Jesus (.66666667) **being full of the Holy Ghost** (full of God 1) Returned from Jordan, and was led by the Spirit into the wilderness" (Luke 4:1). Perhaps, even somewhere in the back of John the Baptist's mind, he heard, "See that you make it according to the pattern that I showed you, after the pattern of the tabernacle, and the pattern of all the instruments thereof, even so shall you make it" (Exodus 25:9). Even so shall you make my Christ? And so he suffered it to be so to fulfill all righteousness and to complete the pattern by baptizing Christ, the Ark of our salvation. You understand that the baptism of the Christ was just a microcosm of the flood, the Christ being the Ark and of course the water representing the great flood.

Furthermore, according to shipbuilders, the ratio of the Ark (300x50x30) represents an advanced knowledge of shipbuilding, since it is the optimum design for stability in rough seas, and that the Ark's design was virtually impossible to capsize, citing that it would have to have been tilted over 90 degrees in order to capsize, due to its balance and proportions. So not only did the ratio carry a message within it, but also it seems that it was the perfect deign for a ship. If we are talking about God, then we are talking about perfection, right? Now, tell me, was that all a coincidence that a man who had probably never been on the seas built the perfect ship, I doubt it? God does not do anything close or just good enough. If He's God, then everything He does is perfect.

So armed with this information, we can now begin to plug this code into all the dimensions that were given to us in the Bible to help us understand why God placed them where He did. All we need to do now is understand the application of each object. From this point on, everything in the Bible that man was instructed to build by a pattern becomes suspect of its allegorical intentions; these things will no longer be a mystery to us now that we have the understanding of our divine ratios. Now, we know what we are looking for, and we know how to equate it.

So as we move along through the book, I will be sure to point out each case of these numbers and their by-products in the Bible. Keep in mind that if we condense the dimensions given to us in the ark, to their lowest common denominators, what we are left with is simply 3s and 5s, which are common dimensional patterns that are found in many of the building projects throughout the Old Testament. From the Brazen Altar to the Ark of the Covenant to the building of Solomon's temple, it is a ratio of numbers; and their variants that can be found in nearly everything, producing that undeniable by-product of 1s and 6s, the future union of God and Christ.

Now we find that in this process of creating such a "biblical" ubiquitous ratio as this one, we need to label it, only so that we can identify it in much quicker terms later on. So in our case, 1.66666667 will become what I like to call the Gamma ratio (Γ), by taking the G from the Greek alphabet to represent God and of course our lower case version (γ) will represent our by-product of .16666667, or its cousin .6666667. As I said, this ratio is quite ubiquitous; not only is it found in the construction of the Ark, but also you can find its influence throughout the construction of the Tabernacle, of which we will explain in depth when we get there. It is also evident in the exchange of money that Joseph and Jesus were both betrayed and sold for. Joseph was sold by his brothers into slavery for 20 pieces of silver, and Jesus was betrayed by Judas for 30. Which when you divide $\frac{20}{30}$ =.66666667, we see that we get the inverse or (γ) of the ratio's by-product, which simply meant that Joseph was a shadow of the Christ to come. In fact, he was the closest one ever created, but he was lacking one thing—the (1). Mind you, it's not that God was not with him, but it's the fact that God was not in him. That was reserved for Christ Himself.

Again, the number's influence does not stop there; as mentioned, it can be found in various other places, all of which I will be sure to try and point out. And, for the skeptical, remember our rule for forming biblical precepts—You need at least three examples in various places to form said rule, right? So again, one example and we can ignore the numbers, two, and we can say "that is interesting," but three or more? Now, we can begin to form our rule that this number with certainty means this or that. So this is our first example; the rest will come later.

With the addition of mathematics to the Bible, it allows us to open another door and go further down the rabbit hole of discovery. And again, it's not that we are inventing anything new here; it is as Immanuel Kant said, "The invented simply becomes the discovered." Meaning that this was always there; it was just waiting for us to discover it. Mathematics should never push us away from the Bible, but instead draw us into it. I think Manly P. Hall summed up mathematics application to our lives and the universe the best when he said:

> In antiquity, the first sciences developed were Astronomy, mathematics and music. But mathematics was the beginning of it all, and the mathematical symbols as developed by the Pythagoreans, was the science of organization. It made possible the classification, an integration of all the different forms of phenomenon in nature. Mathematics enabled us to get the problem of time solved, find locations and to add up various problems and formulas. It is the science of exactitudes; it lifted things out of doubt and generality, which resulted in a formation or a formulization of knowledge. Mathematics took the universal system that we see around us and begun the organization of it, that is, that it did nothing to change the system, **but it organized our concept of the system**, it began to reveal to us the really wonderful universe in which we lived, gradually revealing to us that things were not accidents, but that there were laws and rules governing practically every procedure and function of the universe.

And that is exactly what mathematics does for the Bible; it lifts it out of doubt and generality, and it gives us the ability to organize its concepts, thus revealing to us that things in the Bible are not random and that it's not just a book written by men, but that there are rules and laws that govern it.

> The laws of nature are but the mathematical thoughts of God. (Euclid)

CHAPTER 6

❧

The Resurrection

Purple

> Deep in the human unconscious is a pervasive
> need for a logical universe that makes sense. But
> the real universe is always one step beyond logic.
> (Dune)

One step—Everything seems to be just one step beyond our reach
or our logic, from our universe to that truth that Pilate so ironically
sought for that was right in front of him. And so it seems fitting that
the story of Abraham and his offspring should follow the dictates of
this simple life principle of one step. Why? Because if you have ever
read their story in the Bible, it appears that as much as they wanted
to settle down, God and life would not let them. Even when the Jews
finally built themselves a city, it seems that invading armies were all
too ready to tear it down and ship them off to some distant land.
No other city in the history of the world has been harassed more
than Jerusalem. She has been destroyed at least twice, besieged twen-
ty-three times, attacked fifty-two times, and captured and recaptured
some forty-four times.

But I suppose this is truly the story of life, seeing that we were
not created to be stationary creatures; our lives and our bodies were
designed to be on the move, never static, because we are all just pass-

ing through this life into the next one. It's always just one more step into tomorrow or one more step to whatever, or wherever it is we are going. One more step into heartache, and one more into joy. I guess, by that logic, Adam was always one step away from leaving the Garden, and Noah was, at some point, just one step away from finishing the Ark. And the Christ at some point along the Via Dolorosa had just one more step to take before being nailed to the cross. And yet, as simple as that logic sounds, the one thing on this earth that seems to have managed to stay one step beyond mankind's grasp, and logic, is the Bible. And I suppose until we understand every little facet of it, it will always, partially, remain just out of reach for our finite minds. It truly is difficult for the finite to grasp the infinite.

So, with two parts of the pattern down, we have but one more step to go to the resurrection and, in my opinion, perhaps the easiest one of all to explain. Why? Because it did not involve the use of any physical elements like blood and water, which needed a thorough tearing down to explain the whys. Instead, it uses an element of change to symbolize the resurrection, which fits far better into the realms of symbolism. Why change? Because that's exactly what the whole affair would be for the Christ. It would be a complete and total change for Him, from a physical human state to a spiritual one. Remember that things have to be done much differently in the allegorical realms than in the physical. God could not go around physically killing and resurrecting everyone He wanted to use as a Christ because what would be so special about the actual one coming? So God had to find a way to transmit His message of resurrection by, once again, the limited means of symbolism.

The Covenant of Abraham

And so the Master Weaver strung the work and loomed in His final pattern for humanity. Like a great tapestry being completed, the final thread that pulled the entire pattern together for me was the covenant of Abraham. Once I discovered it and its symbolism, it became very clear to me what God was doing with Abraham in forming the last type to the pattern of Calvary.

You see, when God called Abraham, it was the beginning of the promise that God had made to Adam and Eve long ago in the Garden. What promise? That one day, a deliverer would come and crush the head of the serpent or overcome the death that Adam ushered in. How? Because out of Abraham would come the twelve tribes of Israel, and ultimately, they would produce a great king known as David, and from his linage would come the Christ. He would be the child of that first promise. Now, one could argue that it really all began with Seth, the child born to Adam and Eve after the murder of Abel, whose name means "the appointed one," which implies that out of this son, the promise would come, and of course, it eventually did. But from that time until Abram was called out, that promise had stayed relatively low-key, passing from one person to the next. It wasn't really until God made the covenant with Abram in the wilderness and set the final pattern that the promise truly began to take shape. Why there? Because at that covenant, God would make Abram the first Jew, thus making him the father of all Jews; and the rest is, as they say, history.

Names

Now, since we are breaking down names a bit, I want to take a little side road here to explain the value of names in the Bible. Not only is a name change a significant part of this story, but also some believe that the names in the Bible hold no sway in Biblical interpretations. They believe that the names used are just arbitrary—that somehow it was all just left to chance and God was just working with what He got from man. Believe me, that concept is rubbish.

It's important to understand that names, especially in the Bible, communicate so much more to us than simply a tag or label of what to call someone. They are, in essence, the reputation and the history of who that person was, or was to become, not only to us but also to God. So by God giving names to certain people, or changing them, He would forever establish their reputations, and the whole of those reputations are recalled by the thought or the speaking of those names. There is an entire list of Biblical names that the mere mention of one of them brings into recall an entire life, be it good or bad. Everyone has heard of David and Goliath, and to call a woman a Jezebel is never a positive comment. And so, when we see names in the Bible, it's important to understand that they were inspired by God to project who or what that person was.

Now, for most, when God changed their names, it was to reflect what He had either changed or was about to change in their lives. In essence, their names tell the story of their lives. This is one of the reasons why God changed Abram's name to Abraham. Before receiving the covenant, his first name meant "Exalted father"; but after receiving the promise, God changed his name to Abraham, which means "Father of many," because, again, out of him would come the entire Jewish nation. "No longer shall your name be called Abram, but your name shall be Abraham; for I have made you a father of many nations" (Genesis 17:5). God even went as far as to change his wife's name from Sarai, which meant "My lady," to Sarah, which means "Princess," because she would become the mother of that vast kingdom. God even instructed them to name their only son Isaac, which means "laughter." Why? Because Sarah laughed when she heard she was going to give birth at her age.

So, you see, by changing the names of some people, God was foreshadowing what would happen in their lives; and by giving or inspiring the names of others, He was directing the course of biblical history. This is much like when He sent an angel to Joseph in a dream on Mary's behalf.

> But while he thought on these things, behold, the angel of the Lord appeared unto him in a dream, saying, Joseph, thou son of David, fear not and take unto the Mary thy wife: for that which is conceived in her is of the Holy Ghost. And she shall bring forth a son, and thou shall call his name **Jesus**: for he shall save his people from their sins. (Matthew 1: 20–21)

Now, the name Jesus in Hebrew simply means "salvation" or, as some have said, "Jehovah has become my salvation." The obvious implication here was that He was to become the savior of the world and forever change the course of history. In God's plan, the name had to reflect who and what the child was to become; using just any old name for the savior of the world would not have sufficed. The name was by design, and it was chosen before the world began, as were all the names of all the people who were involved in the Bible

The First Jew

This brings us back to the topic of Abram becoming the first Jew. You see, until that covenant took place, there were no Jews in existence. Abram was just like the rest of the world, an uncircumcised pagan. In fact, there is no indication that he was ever a believer in God until he was called at the age of seventy-five. While we know very little about his life up until this point, we do know that he grew up in a city known as Ur for the first seventy years of his life and, according to tradition, most likely spent those years in his father's idol-making shop. Joshua confirms his pagan roots for us when he said in his speech to the children of Israel at Shechem, "Thus says the Lord God of Israel: 'Your fathers, including Terah, the father of Abraham and the father of Nahor, dwelt on the other side of the River in old times; **and they served other gods**'" (Joshua 24:2).

Now, if you still don't believe that Abram was a nonbeliever, you only need to look as far as the writings of the Jewish historian Flavius Josephus, who does a good job at painting Abram in the same light in his book *Antiquities of the Jews*. He basically explains that Abram was well associated with astronomy and astrology, but that it was by that devotion and close observation to the stars that Abram came to the truth of monotheism (Ant 1.148–256). He also proposed that Abram introduced arithmetic, astronomy, and astrology to the Egyptians.

> He communicated to them arithmetic, and delivered to them the science of astronomy; for before Abram came into Egypt they were unacquainted with those parts of learning; for that science came

from the Chaldeans into Egypt and from thence
to the Greeks also.[2]

In both cases, though, Josephus inserts the idolatrous theme of astronomy/astrology into the biblical account in his attempt to portray Abram's philosophical wisdom and religious genius. Now, we understand that today, astronomy has moved into the field of science and exactitudes, thus leaving behind any mystical attachments; but as for astrology, it has never left those mystical roots.

So again, to call Abram a pagan should not be a stretch; and if that were not enough, one could cite the very city he lived in for seventy years without a calling from God. As for Ur, it was about as idolatrous a place as there ever was. It was part of the Babylonian nation founded some five hundred years before by Nimrod, whose name meant "in opposition to the Lord, or rebel." After his brother Haran's death in Ur, Abram moved with his father Terah and his family to the city of Haran, some 600 miles north of Ur, which was no different than Ur when it came to idolatrous ways because it was still under the influence of the Babylonians.

Now, you might be thinking, didn't they worship God in those cities as well as other gods? As far as I can tell, the answer is no; in fact, the only known city at that time to worship "El Elyon" ("God most high") was the ancient city of Salem, which later became known as Jerusalem, the city of peace, which is said to be one of the oldest postflood cities in the world. According to the Jewish Midrash (rabbinical commentaries directed primarily at the first ten centuries of the Tora), Salem was founded by Noah's son, Shem, who later became known as Melchizedek, which means "my king is righteousness." This is the very one that would later come to bless Abraham after the rescue of his nephew Lot, who, according to biblical records, was still alive at this time. And if you think that Salem was just up the road from Ur or Haran, where Abram could just go and worship at any time, you would be wrong. It appears that Haran was some 658 km from Salem, or 409 mi, and Ur was a short 3157 km, or

---

[2]   (Ant 1.166–168)

roughly 1960 mi from that holy city. However, in closing on Salem, I do think it's quite interesting that they still worship the same god there; it is the only place in the world where they have hung on to their original beliefs.

So needless to say, the Babylonian empire was very wicked, and Ur and Haran were no better. My point to this brief history lesson here is that first, Abram was apparently not a believer and, if he was somehow a believer, it wasn't his only belief; and second, that he came out of a sinful situation much like Noah did. But don't get distracted by the fact that Abram was an idol maker or a nonbeliever; that's irrelevant, seeing that he answered the call of God when prompted to is the primary objective to the story.

The Calling Out

And this is yet another typical biblical pattern that needs pointing out. That God always calls His men that were to be in the image of His Son out of sinful times or situations, as the Christ Himself would be called from such a time. It is the same situation as when God calls any person out of the world and converts them to His ways. You will see this time and time again throughout the stories of the Bible, where God calls, then leads out to some remote area, and then finishes His work on that person, only to lead them back to become a deliverer. You can find this pattern in nearly every major Bible story from Abram to Jacob and from Joseph to Moses to Joshua; in fact, we even find that King David was subject to this unseen force. We first see him anointed to be king of Israel by Samuel and then fleeing for his life from Saul the current king, until such time that God saw fit to bring him back as the new king and deliverer of Israel at the age of 30. You see, David couldn't begin his kingship until that time because Christ would not start His ministry until He was 30. Keep this number in mind because we will be examining it later.

Now, the allegory or the point to this whole process is to reflect that one day, God would call His Son from among men, "But when the fullness of the time had come, God sent forth His Son, born of a woman, born under the law" (Galatians 4:4). He would be born and subject to the flesh, thus the reasoning behind calling men out of dark sinful situations. The leading out into remote locations is symbolic of the death and term of burial of the Christ; in essence, it is a symbol of spiritual purification through separation from the world; and the returning as a deliverer is of course symbolic of the Christ resurrecting and breaking the yoke of sin and death that has held the world in bondage. And again, it is a good display of God's use of the macro- and the microcosm. It is always patterns inside of patterns and wheels inside of wheels, and we will explore it often along our journey to the crucifixion.

So, understanding this pattern now, it is easy to see that when God finally did call Abram out of Haran, it was to create that separation that was needed for God to complete His work and mold him in the image of His Son.

> Now, the Lord had said to Abram: "Get out of your country, from your family and from your father's house, to a land that I will show you. I will make you a great nation; I will **bless** you and make your name great; and you shall be a blessing. I will bless those who bless you, and I will curse him who curses you; and in you all the families of the earth shall be **blessed**." (Genesis 12:1–3)

The other reason for removing Abram from his homeland was so that the influences of that idolatrous culture could no longer effect or interfere with what He was about to do in his life.

The Blood

So Abram left his father's house and took with him his wife, Sarai, and his nephew, Lot. Like all that would make that leap of faith and abandon all to follow God, Abram was no different in the fact that he had no clue as to where God was taking him or just how God would use him to create the final portion of the pattern. But before Abram could get to the promise of that blessing, he would, much like Noah his predecessor, have to fulfill the initial portions of the pattern concerning the blood and the water.

You see, when Abram left, it wasn't too far before we find him building an altar and sacrificing to the Lord, thus fulfilling that one unwritten law of worship and shadowing the crucifixion of the Christ through the shedding of that innocent blood.

> Abram passed through the land to the place of Shechem, as far as the terebinth tree of Moreh. And the Canaanites were then in the land. Then the Lord appeared to Abram and said, "To your descendants I will give this land." And there he built an altar to the Lord, who had appeared to him. And he moved from there to the mountain east of Bethel, and he pitched his tent with Bethel on the west and Ai on the east; there he built an **altar** to the Lord and called on the name of the Lord. (Genesis 12:7–8)

Now, this wasn't the only place that the Bible records Abram sacrificing upon altars along his journey to that promise. After his expedition into Egypt, he returns to his first altar and sacrifices there again.

> And he went on his journey from the South as far as Bethel, to the place where his tent had been at the beginning, between Bethel and Ai, to the place of the **altar** which he had made there at first. And there Abram **called** on the name of the Lord. (Genesis 13:3–4)

And again after he separates from his nephew Lot, after God speaks to him concerning the promise:

> Arise, walk in the land through its length and its width, for I give it to you. Then Abram moved

his tent, and went and dwelt by the terebinth trees of Mamre, which are in Hebron, and built an **altar** there to the Lord. (Genesis 13:17–18)

Now, keep in mind that when altars were built in the biblical context, they were always for a sacrifice; and in Abram's case, it would be no different. Blood was needed to fulfill the type.

The Water

Now, I said that Abram would have to fulfill both of our former types; and even though the Bible does not say it openly, it is a very well-known biblical fact that along Abram's journey to that promised land, he had to cross many rivers, thus fulfilling our second type concerning the burial of the Christ. As I said before, the second portion always involved the use of water in some fashion. So how do I know Abram crossed rivers?" Well, besides the many maps that are available charting his journeys, the first clue of this is given to us in the Bible where Abram is called a Hebrew.

They also took Lot, Abram's brother's son who dwelt in Sodom, and his goods, and departed. Then one who had escaped came and told Abram **the Hebrew**, for he dwelt by the terebinth trees of Mamre the Amorite, brother of Eshcol and brother of Aner; and they were allies with Abram. (Genesis 14:12–13)

That word Hebrew is the confirmation that Abram fulfilled the second portion of the pattern by crossing the water of many rivers. I used to think that the term Hebrew was just another way of saying Jew, but I understood that this could not be right because Abram had not yet received the covenant of the circumcision. So how could he be called a Jew when there were none in existence? Simple, because the word is not a race-related term, but an action-related one, and it is the first clue that ties Abram to the water element of the pattern.

You see, the word "Hebrew" in the Jewish language is עברי (Ivrie). The root letters mean to cross over, or pass through, literally expressing the ideal of one or someone traversing, passing, or crossing over something. From what I could gather from various sources in the biblical context, it seems to have primarily referred to those who have traversed rivers. Thus, of course, our symbolic meaning becomes much clearer when we understand the term and Abram's journeys. When he first left Ur, he crossed the Euphrates River at least twice on his way to Haran. Then, when he received the call from God, he crossed the Euphrates River again and the Jordan River to get to Shechem. From Shechem, he traveled to Bethel; and from Bethel, he went to Egypt, where he would have crossed over the Nile River going in and going out. And finally, he settled in Hebron or Mamre as it's called in the Bible. So it appears that Abram was crossing rives as much as he was building altars.

Again, Joshua gives us this account of events and a clue to how the descendants of Abram became known as Hebrews:

> Thus says the Lord, the God of Israel, "Long ago, your fathers lived beyond the Euphrates, Terah, the father of Abraham and of Nahor; and they served other gods. Then I took your father Abraham from beyond the **River** and led him through all the land of Canaan, and made his offspring many... Then I brought your fathers out of Egypt, and you came to the **sea**. And the Egyptians pursued your fathers with chariots and horsemen to the Red Sea... Then I brought you to the land of the Amorites, who lived on the other side of the **Jordan**. They fought with you, and I gave them into your hand"...
>
> Now therefore fear the Lord and serve him in sincerity and in faithfulness. Put away the gods that your fathers served **beyond the River** and in Egypt, and serve the Lord. And if it is evil in your eyes to serve the Lord, choose this day whom you

will serve, whether the gods your fathers served in the region **beyond the River**, or the gods of the Amorites in whose land you dwell. But as for me and my house, we will serve the Lord. (Joshua 24:2–15)

As you can see, these Hebrew have done quite a bit of water crossings, from Abram when he departed from Ur until he settled down in Hebron to the Exodus and the Red Sea crossing and then the entry into the Promised Land as they crossed over the Jordan River. For Joshua, the symbolism was clear—on one side of the river is idol worship, but we have left that life behind when we crossed over to the other side. Now, we will serve the Lord in a symbolically resurrected lifestyle. Rest assured that we will explore each of these cases in detail when we get to them, but the allegory for now follows the pattern exactly. It is always blood first and then water, a death and then a burial; the pattern never deviates. Now, you might be thinking, where was the sacrifice for Abram when he left Haran, because his first blood sacrifice was in Bethel? I mean, if were keeping to the pattern, then there should have been a sacrifice before he began his journey following God, right? True, but his first real sacrifice was not one of blood, but one of self-will.

You see, when Abram received his calling from God, he repented, or turned from serving those false gods of his past and turned to serve the living God, which is of course symbolic of sacrifice, or death, a quintessential dying out to that former life. Just as the Christ would utter that famous line in the garden before His death, "not my will but thine," He died out or repented just as Abram did before Him. Then, Abram would have crossed the Euphrates River to symbolize the burial of the Christ and his former life, which then would have thrust him into his wonderings and isolation to symbolize the term of that burial in the tomb and remaining ever faithful, looking for the day that God would give him the promise and resurrect him, from his isolation, and fulfill the shadow of the Christ conquering the grave.

And so one day, God would finally come to Abram to fulfill the promise He had made to him some twenty-four years ago. This is the promise that would involve an act that would separate Abram and his people from the rest of the world; it would set them apart forever as God's unique people and ultimately establish the final portion of the pattern.

The Covenant

When Abram was ninety-nine years old, the Lord appeared to him and said, "I am Almighty God; walk before me and be blameless. And I will make my covenant between me and you, and will multiply you exceedingly." Then, Abram fell on his face, and God talked with him, saying:

> As for me, behold, my covenant is with you, and you shall be a father of many nations. No longer shall your name be called **Abram**, but your name shall be **Abraham**; for I have made you a father of many nations. I will make you exceedingly fruitful; and I will make nations of you, and kings shall come from you. And I will establish my covenant between me and you and your descendants after you in their generations, for an everlasting covenant, to be God to you and your descendants after you . . .
>
> And God said to Abraham: "As for you, you shall keep my covenant, you and your descendants after you throughout their generations. "This is the covenant that you and your descendants must keep: each male among you **must be circumcised**; the flesh of his foreskin **must be** cut off. This will be a **sign** that you and they have **accepted** this **covenant**. Every male child must be circumcised on the eighth day after his birth. This applies not only to members of your fam-

ily, but also to the servants born in your household and the foreign-born servants from you have purchase. **Your bodies will thus bear the mark of my everlasting covenant**. Anyone who refuses to be circumcised **will be cut off** from the covenant family for violating the covenant. (Genesis 17: 9-14)

Now, if you are the legal-minded type, then you can't help but notice all the legal ramifications existing in this covenant, or contract. When you see the word "**must**" or "sign that you have **accepted**" and especially "you **will** be cut off," these are legally binding words, meaning that once you agree, you are bound by the terms of the contract to perform said obligations or face the consequences of the contract. And I might add that it was binding both ways, for Abraham and God. On Abraham's side, he would have to be circumcised; and on God's side, he would have to maintain the blessings.

Now, I want you to notice that God mentioned twice that this was "an everlasting covenant." Meaning, this covenant was not ever going away; it was as the term says, "everlasting," just like Noah's covenant with the rainbow; and these covenants, like the rest, will be with us until time is no more. Now, the consequences of not fulfilling this covenant seem pretty drastic for the one who is not circumcised; at first glance, most people just read on by and don't recognize the uniqueness of what's happening here, but there are a few things that need to be brought to light.

The first is that God said, "It would be a token." Now, a token, as defined by Webster's dictionary, means:

> An outward sign of expression, a symbol or emblem, a distinguishing feature, a souvenir or keepsake, a small part representing the whole, something given or shown as a guarantee (as of authority, right or identity). Done or given as a token in partial fulfillment of an obligation or engagement, a payment.

So the circumcision was definitely an outward sign or expression to the covenant asked by God because it would be the removal of the outer foreskin. That would become quite the distinguishing feature that would set them apart from the rest of the world, in essence creating the divide between the clean and the unclean. Remember that God is always concerned with cleanliness, both physically and spiritually. The circumcision would also be a small symbolic part representing the whole of the promise in the future, of which Abraham could not yet see. And it would be an outward sign of what God was going to do in the future on the inside of man; it would be a guarantee by God that He would perform a circumcision one day that was made without hands upon the hearts of man. "And the Lord your God will **circumcise your heart**, and the **heart of your seed**, to love the Lord your God with all your heart, and with all your soul, that you may live forever" (Deuteronomy 30:6).

That verse of scripture is one of the reasons why this would be an everlasting covenant because this was a glimpse into the future of what Calvary would actually do for humanity. Calvary would allow God access to the hearts of men through faith in His Son. Now, many have suggested that Calvary did away with all such contracts; but, again, this was everlasting. Now, I'm not sure what your definition of everlasting is; but with God, it means forever. So what happened to these contracts? Nothing. They were simply changed. Calvary moved these covenants from external actions to internal actions, and the scriptures support this idea as we read, "When you came to Christ, you were circumcised, but not by a physical procedure. It was a spiritual procedure-the cutting away of your sinful nature" (Colossians 2:11). Man had to symbolically do what God could not do in the spirit because of the barrier of sin; but, after Calvary, that barrier was removed, and the Spirit of God could now enter into man and perform that spiritual procedure. This is what the day of Pentecost was all about—It was God fulfilling His obligation to mankind by giving the gift of the Holy Spirit and circumcising the hearts of man. And that would be the day that the promise was fulfilled that God had made to Abraham so long ago: Out of him, all the nations of the earth would be blessed.

So you see, the symbolism behind this whole affair served a twofold message. One was to reflect that God would move the soon-coming Law from the tablets of stone that they were first written on to the tables of men's hearts. The symbolic implication is that stone is unbendable; if pressured, it breaks; but if the Law could be written on the newly circumcised hearts of men, then it would have flexibility and mercy. Ezekiel pointed out this very concept.

> Then I will sprinkle clean water upon you, and you will be clean: from all your filthiness, and from all your idols, I will cleanse you. **A new heart also will I give you**, and **a new spirit will I put within you**: and I will **take away the stony heart out of your flesh, and I will give you a heart of flesh**. And **I will put my Spirit within you**, and cause you to walk in my statutes, and you shall keep my judgments, and do them. (Ezekiel 36:25–27)

God was, of course, speaking of the day that the Christ would rise from the grave and usher in that new and living way; that's why this was a symbol of the resurrection. God could not, nor would not, change the old covenant until the Christ had risen from the grave and established the new one. This is the very thing that Jeremiah was writing about.

> Behold, the days are coming, says the Lord, when **I will make a new covenant** with the house of Israel and with the house of Judah, **not according to the covenant** that I made with their fathers in the day that I took them by the hand to lead them **out of the land of Egypt** (aka the stone tablets), my covenant which they broke, though I was a husband to them, says the Lord. But **this is**

> **the covenant** that I will make with the house of
> Israel **after those days** (Calvary), says the Lord: **I
> will put my law** in **their minds**, and **write it on
> their hearts**; and I will be their God, and they
> shall be my people. (Jeremiah 31: 31–33)

So keep in mind that the covenant never changed; it was simply relocated. And not only would this be a changing or morphing of covenants, but also it would be a change for the Christ. As I said earlier, His resurrection would be the changing point from the dead to the living, from the bound unclean flesh that bore the sins of the world to the grave to the unbound clean spirit set loose from the bonds of mortality. This is why the circumcision was an allegory of the resurrection of the Christ. It was symbolic of what would be spiritually cut away when He rose from the grave.

So now, you understand that the foreskin was just a symbol, a shadow, nothing more of what God was going to do in the future. It was just another allegory pointing the way to Calvary. And the second symbolic portion of the circumcision was what it would actually do for humanity—the cutting away of our unbending hearts of stone by the entering in of His Spirit and giving us malleable hearts of flesh. This is why God said that He will put "a new spirit within you." It is our rebirth, our resurrection from the physical bonds of life, and a transformation to one enabled by the Spirit of God until we can be made like Christ.

As I said, the promise of the circumcision was to be symbolic of a transformation; for Abraham, it would be the thing that set him apart from the rest of the world, transforming him from unclean to clean. This is why he went from Abram to Abraham; God transformed him to conform to the pattern of the death, burial, and resurrection of His Son. You see, Abraham died to that former life when he left home, was buried when he crossed the rivers, and was resurrected when he received the circumcision—pattern complete. As for the Christ, it would be the cutting off of the weakness of the physical and the hardness of death, removing all of its sin-tainted flaws, and setting the Christ free into a new life by the power of God's Spirit.

Again, change was to be the driving factor in the shaping of the pattern that a metamorphosis occurs symbolically.

So, with the circumcision of Abraham, God completed His pattern of Calvary for the time being; however, due to the time separation between Adam and Eve to Noah and then to Abraham, the pattern still wasn't very clear. There was too much of a time gap for man to comprehend what was going on, but rest assured, God was about to tighten the pattern up. There were still some things and people that had parts to play in fulfilling God's pattern of Calvary. But for the remainder of the Bible, from this point on, when we come across a transformation, or as I like to call it the miraculous, it will be symbolic of this future resurrection. Now, the pattern is complete; we can follow it to its ending by simply picking up its tracks—It is blood, then water, and then the miraculous. It is repentance, then a water crossing, and then a transformation. It's a symbolic death, burial, and resurrection. Now begins the process of narrowing the types that would set the pattern even further. But it is these three types that form the foundation of the pattern of Calvary—the death with Adam and Eve, the burial with Noah, and the resurrection with Abraham. After this, the pattern becomes more complex in its designs, yet remains relatively easy to understand.

In closing, I think it's sad that we have drifted so far from these core ideas and symbols of the Bible that they appear new to us now, but thank God, they are not lost. No longer will we be separated by ideologies and dogmas of narrow-minded religions. Mind you, we are not changing anything fundamental here. We are simply adding a broader database that facilitates an ease of thinking: "The children born tomorrow will all understand what we're talking about today" (Robert Kaplan).

> My father once told me that respect for truth comes close to being the basis for all morality. "Something cannot emerge from nothing," he said. This is profound thinking if you understand how unstable "the truth" can be. (Dune)

CHAPTER 7

The God of Abraham, Isaac, and Jacob

The God of the pattern

> Must then a Christ perish in torment in every age
> to save those who have no imagination? (George
> Bernard Shaw)

I'm not sure if Shaw wrote this line with the understanding of the repetitive patterns of the Bible, seeing those Messiah figures come and go between the pages with their repeated attempts to wake the sleeping masses. The likelihood of that is quite slim. More than likely, it was directed to those brave few that seem to come along every so often to stand against the tyranny of the day and sacrificially lay down their lives, all so that others might wake up and believe in their cause. For those few, it is all about liberation from something, be it tyranny or slavery or, yes, even sin. There is something about oppression that some men cannot stand, while others file blindly into the pens as bleating sheep. I believe that's why Shaw posed the question that way—It was easy for him to relate the struggles of those few to that of the Christ and His struggles. In essence, that was the Christ's primary objective: He came to deliver humanity from all forms of oppression because, in reality, they are all one and the same.

Oppression is oppression, no matter how you dress it up; and there will always be the few that will stand up for the many who have no imagination, to lead the way and set the captives free.

So now that we have established the foundation of Calvary and its elemental attributes with the blood, the water, and what I like to call the miraculous, which, again, is that evident change in an event or a life, let's move on because, as you can imagine, God didn't stop there. The Master Weaver still had many more Calvaries to thread into the lives of men and the pages of the Bible. Now, from this point on, the chapters will become increasingly more complex, especially when we get to the actual Law and the Tabernacle; but as you will see, they are all built on the same symbolic principles. It is just that they will require a little more ferreting out.

But, then again, that's really what it is all about, isn't it? It's about discovery, no matter how difficult the road. Somewhere down that road lays the answers to why God did the things He did. In order for us to travel that path, we will have to keep introducing new concepts in our continued assault on those old dogmatic walls that have limited our view of the Bible and its information. As any student of history knows, the reasoning behind building walls is fear; walls are a fortification against the unknown because the unknown often brings change. It is that fear of change that is perhaps the most overwhelming force to the whole concept of being dogmatic because, oftentimes, attached to that change is the realization that one has been wrong in their assumptions, and nobody like to be wrong.

And because of that, changing someone's point of view is one of the most difficult things a person can do. Oh sure, you can feed most people new concepts and ideas all day long, and they can embrace those at a moderate rate, as long as they do not interfere with their foundational beliefs. But try to change someone's perceived view of truth, and, look out, you have a fight on your hands. Why? Because truth, especially in a religious context, is often subjective, meaning that it exists in the mind of the individual, rather than the object of thought and hard analytical proof. Just because someone says it is truth doesn't make it so. One only has to look as far as Jim Jones and David Koresh to prove that last statement.

So every claimed truth has to be substantiated; it has to be established on concrete evidence in order for it to truly be considered truth. As I like to say, 2+2 will always be 4, no matter where you go in the universe because it has been validated by numerous mathematicians, and we ourselves have instituted it throughout our world view as factual; therefore, it is truth. So, when I say we are on a mission of discovery, this is exactly what I mean: We are searching for a biblical truth that is concrete, that cannot be untold or undone by someone else's version of their perceived truth. We are literally bound by obligation of the truth to go beyond those walls of dogma and set our sights on the vast unknown regions of the Bible.

This brings us back to the fact that changing people's perceived truth is one of the hardest things to do because accepting an alternate reality means changing everything about their universe surrounding their current views. For example, if you were taught your entire life that 2+2=5, then that is truth, regardless of the fact that it equals 4, because it still exists as truth in your mind, that is, until either you discover an alternate version on your own or someone else provides enough evidence to prove that 2+2 really equals 4. It is at that point that the person is left with one of two decisions—either ignore the facts and live life as normal, which most do, taking that symbolically passive "blue pill," or accept the fact that their version of perceived truth was wrong and take the "red pill," which changes their paradigm forever.

In which case, it often comes with a very high price, usually the rejection of their peers and an expulsion from their known environment. And it is that option of change that classifies people into two categories that I like to call intellectually dishonest and intellectually honest. Some can admit it, and some cannot, and unfortunately, it will always be that way; for some strange reason, some people cannot embrace truth. Understand that there is no in between with truth—either you are in or you are not. "This is profound thinking if you understand how unstable 'the truth' can be" (Dune).

Truth is not always welcome because it has the ability to change so much in such a short amount of time. Again, one should never accept the taught truth until they have proven it themselves; only then can one truly say, "I am on the right path." So, if you're ready to follow the white rabbit a little further down the hole, then let's begin. But remember that if you're unsure, you can always turn back. But then again, you will never know just how deep the hole goes. I hope you are ready, Alice.

The God of Abraham, Isaac, and Jacob

So, have you ever wondered why God often made the statement in the Bible, "I am the God of Abraham, the God of Isaac and the God of Jacob?" I mean, He could have said it about so many other people; yet when we see Him saying it, it is almost as if He's beaming with pride at these words, letting the reader know that He is the God of these great patriarchs. Well, there is a reason for this. It is because they were the ones that God would once again establish another pattern of Calvary through. They were the ones I like to call the typesetters.

This is one of the reasons why God mentioned the phrase so often, because wrapped up in the lives of those three men existed, if only in symbolic form, the death, burial, and resurrection. This is why God used them and held them in such high esteem: They yielded to the will of God in the shaping of their lives, and for that trust, they would forever be a part of God's grand design. But enough of that; let me show you how they fulfilled the pattern in the course of their lives.

Altars

First, let me ask you a question, what was Abraham known for doing throughout his journeys in the Bible? Building altars. Abraham was always building altars. Why? Well, the obvious and topical reason was because, at that time, the building of altars and the sacrifices performed upon them was really the only set form of worship to God, and, of course, the underlying meaning was directed toward that future sacrifice of the Christ as we have already established. And just a little side note here, keep in mind that there was no Mosaic

Law established at this time. These sacrifices were the implied remediation for sin. This was not a written code, but rather a verbal code, a tradition that was passed down from Adam and Eve, which stood with the force of Law until the actual Law would come and formally enforce it because if you will notice with me, in each case of Abraham's sacrifices, they were done to worship God, not to atone for sin.

And let's be clear on this point because it will culminate in Calvary later on, but when I mention "altars," I am not only referring to the various structures themselves but also the blood sacrifices that were committed upon them. In fact, there is only one event that I'm aware of that occurred upon an altar where oil was used instead of blood, and that was with Jacob in his journeys.

Now, just in case you're not sure what an altar really is in the Biblical context, let me give you a basic understanding before we move on. Webster defines it as:

> A usually raised structure or place on which sacrifices are offered or incense is burned in worship—often used figuratively to describe a thing given great or undue precedence or value especially at the cost of something else.

But that's kind of a general explanation. The Holman Bible Dictionary gives us a little deeper break down on altars, stating that:

> The Hebrew word for altar that is used most frequently in the Old Testament is formed from the verb for slaughter and means literally, "slaughter place." Altars were used primarily as places of sacrifice, especially animal sacrifice.
>
> While animals were a common sacrifice in the Old Testament, altars were also used to sacrifice grain, fruit, wine, and incense (this would come with the introduction of the Law). The grain and fruit sacrifices were offered as a tithe

of the harvest or as representative first fruits of the harvest. They were presented in baskets to the priest who set the basket before the altar (Deuteronomy 26:2–4). Wine was offered along with animal and bread sacrifices. Incense was burned on altars to purify after slaughtering's and to please God with sweet fragrance.

In the Old Testament, altars are distinguished by the material used in their construction. The simplest altars, and perhaps oldest, were the earthen altars (Exodus 20:24). This type of altar was made of either mud-brick or a raised roughly shaped mound of dirt. The stone altar is the most commonly mentioned altar in biblical records and the most frequently found in excavations from Palestine. A single large stone could serve as an altar (Judges 6:19–23; Judges 13:19–20; 1 Samuel 14:31–35). Similarly, unhewn stones could be carefully stacked to form an altar (Exodus 20:25, 1 Kings 18:30–35). Such stone altars were probably the most common form of altar prior to the building of the Solomon's Temple.

Now, I realize we all have our modern concepts of altars; but even when we combine them with these definitions, you can't help but come away with a clinical feeling to the whole thing; definitions cannot transmit the feelings and emotions that surrounded the art of sacrifice. Furthermore, they lack the ability to transmit what they meant to God and just how important this whole process was to Him. The altars were places of deep heartfelt devotion and, oftentimes, considerable effort. One did not build an altar just to build one; with the laying of each stone, there would have been considerable thought placed into it. Just look at the consideration that Elijah placed into the building of the altar when facing the prophets of Baal:

> Then Elijah said to all the people, "Come near to me." So all the people came near to him. And he repaired the altar of the Lord that was broken down. And Elijah **took twelve stones, according to the number of the tribes of the sons of Jacob**, to whom the word of the Lord had come, saying, "Israel shall be your name." Then with the stones he built an altar in the name of the Lord. (1 Kings 18:30–32)

These were places of intense worship because they were meant to mirror the intensity that would culminate at Calvary. Sacrifice was anything but trivial. Death is never a trivial thing; taking a life is never easy, even if it is to eat. For this reason, God told Moses,

> For the **life** of the flesh **is in the blood**, and I have given it to you upon **the altar to make atonement for your souls**; for **it is the blood that makes atonement for the soul**. Therefore I said to the children of Israel, "No one among you shall eat blood, nor shall any stranger who dwells among you eat blood." (Leviticus 17:11–12)

And there's the keyword, "atonement," which translated means "to make reconciliation." That's what the blood of the sacrifice accomplished upon the altar: It reconciled or restored the offender's soul to God. But again, what we miss is that each time a sacrifice was offered upon the altar, God was looking into the future, toward that day that His only Son would be sacrificed upon the altar of the cross. Can you imagine what that must have been like, to see all of those thousands of sacrifices that transpired throughout time, knowing that one day that was going to be your only Son in that place? For us, that would be like having the same nightmare not just every night for the rest of your life, but for your entire life. And that's the intensity that surround the sacrifices at the altar and what it all meant to God every time it happened; it literally forced Him to look ahead to that day. That's why He was so adamant about the sacrifices being perfect; they had to measure up to the value of His Son. If it was going to be your son, wouldn't you want those symbolic sacrifices to be perfect as well, to reflect just how much he meant to you? Again, there was nothing trivial going on at the altar; it was a place of the utmost importance.

So you see there was a much deeper and far more complex relationship happening between the altars and the sacrifices than it seems we formerly thought. They were the places of restoration for humanity and the foreshadowing of the Christ's death. However, due in large part to the fact that we no longer partake in animal sacrifice, we have become dispassionate observers to the whole process, and we don't really see the value today. I mean, can you imagine having to depend upon a sacrifice to reconcile you to God every time you messed up? The value that you would place on that animal would be far beyond our concepts of cost today. It would be in relation to your soul, and how do you put a value on that? What's the cost, a million, ten million? Where's the upper limit for selling your soul to eternal damnation? So knowing that, how does one go about placing a value on just one of these sacrificial animals? The answer is, you can't, but yet it is still put upon us to understand the relationship between God, the altar, and the blood sacrifice to really get a true understanding of not only the importance to the performer of the act but also what Christ would accomplish at Calvary through His bloody death. Look, if the sacrificing of animals was able to reconcile the souls of men to God at that time, how much more shall the blood of Christ reconcile us today?

My point is that we have a tendency to just read over the story, but never grasp the magnitude of what was really happening. These were such unique and special places to humanity because they were the symbols of man's willing devotion to clear the way between him and God. This was not exclusive to just the Hebrews, either. Blood sacrifices transpired throughout every culture; we all have our roots in blood. In pagan cultures, they would often construct these elaborate altars in the likeness of their deities and then sacrifice their own children upon these altars; that's how important it was for early man to reconcile himself to the gods. If they could do that, then why not sacrifice animals to God?

But no matter where the altars stood, they were the places where the innocent came to die for the sins of the guilty. It has been a constant theme throughout history that reaches all the way to Calvary and beyond. Blood alone turns the pages of the Bible and writes its history. "And according to the law almost all things are purified with blood, and without shedding of blood there is no remission" (Hebrews 9:22).

Abraham

So very briefly, let's revisit Abraham's journeys and his altar building once more. Hidden in among that story of building altars and crossing rivers is the foundation for the start of the next pattern. Wheels within wheels, right? So while he was being led through one pattern, another had already begun; and if you will notice, nearly every time Abraham built an altar, it was directly after an encounter with God. Now, he might have built altars in between these times; we are not really sure on that because we are dealing with limited information and, of course, a nearly 4000-year gap. But these encounters obviously warranted the need to honor the God that was directing his life in the pattern of Calvary. In fact, Abraham's life was modeled so much after Calvary that he even took his only son Isaac up Mount Moriah to sacrifice him, which unknowingly would be fulfilling another type.

> So Abram departed as the Lord had spoken to him, and Lot went with him. And Abram was seventy-five years old when he departed from Haran. He took his wife, Sari, his nephew Lot, and all his wealth- his livestock and all the people who had joined his household at Haran-and finally arrived in Canaan. Traveling through Canaan, for the area was inhabited by Canaanites. Then the Lord appeared to Abraham and said, "I am going to

give this land to you and your offspring." And
Abraham built an **altar** there to commemorate
the Lord's visit. (Genesis 12:4–7)

Again, that was the first altar that he built to honor God's
promise of the future; the next he built seemingly soon after, when
he made the short 20-mile trip from Shechem to Bethel: "After
that, Abram traveled southward and set up camp in the hill country
between Bethel on the west and Ai on the east. There he built an
altar and worshiped the Lord" (Genesis 12:8).

Then a famine was in the land and forced him to go out to
Egypt and back again, and upon his journey back to the same area,
he stopped at the altar he previously built in Bethel and worshiped
God:

And he went on his journeys from the South even
to Bethel, unto the place where his tent had been
at the beginning, between Bethel and Ai; unto
the place of the **altar**, which he had made there
at the first: and there Abram called on the name
of the Lord. (Genesis 13:3–4)

Now again, here we have the beginning of a very faint shadow
that we will run into quite often in our journey, and that is this
coming out of Egypt theme. Abraham was the first to do it, and then
when Joseph is sold into slavery and finds himself serving in Egypt,
he mandates to the people that upon their leaving Egypt, they are to
take his bones with them. And of course, there was Moses, who was
raised in Egypt and then departed, only to return again as a Messiah
figure and lead the people out in the great Exodus. Now, there is a
reason for this, which of course was centered on the Christ, but we
will have to get to that later.

So then, the next one came after Abraham's separation from his
nephew Lot:

And I am going to give you so many descendants that, like dust, they cannot be counted. Take a walk in every direction and explore the new possessions I am giving you. Then Abram moved his camp to the Oak Grove owned by Mamre, which is at Hebron. There he built an **altar** to the Lord. (Genesis 13:16–18)

Again, we see Abraham building an altar dedicated to a future promise, all the while never really understanding that those sacrifices were in the shadow of the future promise of Christ to come. The final altar I would like to point out was with his son Isaac:

And he said, take now your son, your only son Isaac, whom you love, and get thee into the land of Moriah; and offer him there for a burnt offering upon one of the mountains which I will tell thee of. And Abraham rose up early in the morning and saddled his donkey and took two of his young men with him, and Isaac his son, clave the word for the burnt offering, and rose up, and they came to the place which God had told him of; and Abraham built an **altar** there, and laid the wood in order, and bound Isaac his son, and laid him on the altar upon the wood. (Genesis 22: 2–9)

Undoubtedly grief-stricken at God's request to sacrifice his only son, we see that Abraham gathered up the necessary things and departed for what I'm sure was the most difficult task of his life. Now contrary to what we might think, by the writings of the Bible and other sources, it seems that Isaac did not even resist. It appears that Isaac willingly gave of himself to be sacrificed, much in the fashion that Christ would. This makes sense. I mean, if you're going to model things after Calvary, then why not get them as close as you can to type? In fact, I believe it was Josephus in Antiquity of the Jews who said:

> Now Isaac was of such a generous disposition as became the son of such a father, and was pleased with this discourse; and said, "That he was not worthy to be born at first, if he should reject the determination of God and of his father, and should not resign himself up readily to both their pleasures; since it would have been unjust if he had not obeyed, even if his father alone had so resolved." So he went immediately to the altar to be sacrificed. And the deed had been done if God had not opposed it; for he called loudly to Abraham by his name, and forbade him to slay his son; and said, "It was not out of a desire of human blood that he was commanded to slay his son, nor was he willing that he should be taken away from him whom he had made his father, but to try the temper of his mind, whether he would be obedient to such a command."

But thank God He sent an angel to stay the hand of Abraham because, as I've heard somewhere else, "Isaac was as good as dead in the mind of Abraham." And so this ends Abraham's record of building altars. Though it may seem short, these events took place over a vast amount of time; in fact, when Abraham died, he was 175 years old, which means that this transpired over the course of a hundred years.

Now, my point to this little piece of redundancy is that not only was Abraham moving symbolically vertical toward the resurrection in his life with the covenant of the circumcision, but also, at the same time, he was moving linear or in an outward fashion toward the next pattern with those altars, thus once again laying the foundation stone of the death of the Christ. Why? Because what he built on here, his son and grandson would complete. They would be the ones who would continue the movement along that Z axis, which is the axis that moves diagonal to everything else and places the depth in the object of design. And it is these kinds of things about the Bible that simply amaze me: How God could be building one pattern, all the while starting the next one within the one He is building. I mean, if you consider the complexity of the writings, not only is God writing on the x, y, and z axis, but also He was writing on that axis that is in the future, the one that puts the fourth dimensional angle on the pattern; and what is the axis of that? How do you compute writing on that scale? It is no wonder this has remained hidden for so long. How could ancient man ever figure this out? The more you zoom in this microscope, the more you see the pattern, and the more you begin to realize that that is what the whole Bible was constructed around—These highly complex multidimensional symbolic foretellings of the Christ to come and the process by which He would suffer for the sins of the world, thus making reconciliation with His perfect blood upon that altar we call the cross.

Just look at the symbolism that surrounded the sacrifice of Isaac, and you will see that God had a plan for everything. Not only did this allegory display a loving father sacrificing his only son, as God would do with the Christ, but also it was a three-day journey for Abraham and Isaac to Mount Moriah, which was the same amount of time that the Christ would be buried in the tomb. That three-day journey acted as the symbolic burial of Christ because from the time God told Abraham to sacrifice his only son, Isaac was as good as dead in the eyes of his father. These must have been the hardest three days of Abraham's life. While Isaac was alive for those three days, in his father's mind, he was dead. But even there lies a bit of truth because, in the eyes of God, was the Christ ever really dead? Did He ever leave the sight of the Father? No, of course not, so then this story dovetails perfectly into the pattern.

Keep in mind, though, that this will not be the only time that we will explore the duration of a journey to ferret out an allegory. The other thing I would like to point out is the use of the number three again, which is the number of birth and rebirth, which is actually what it would be for Isaac when the ram was found in the thicket. And the last, but surely not the least, the allegorical message that was hidden in the verse where Abraham tells Isaac that God will provide the offering.

> Then he (Isaac) said, "Look, the fire and the wood, but where is the lamb for a burnt offering?" And Abraham said, "My son, **God will provide for Himself the lamb** for a burnt offering." So the two of them went together. (Genesis 22:7–8)

And there's the key message to this whole allegory: It is that God will provide not only a substitution for Isaac but also, one day, for the entire world, when Christ would become the ram caught in the thicket of humanity's sins. As John the Baptist said, "Behold! The Lamb of God who takes away the sin of the world!" (John 1:29)

I find it interesting that, in the last recorded sacrifice of Abraham's life, we find him with his son completing the pattern once more in a very infantile stage of its development. We see that Isaac is killed the moment God tells Abraham to sacrifice him and then the three-day journey acting as the burial, only to find that at the end of the allotted time, Isaac is resurrected by God and is literally and symbolically born again. Isaac was truly the first open vision of the Christ, so much so that it is quite uncanny how much of that event symbolically fits into the lens of Calvary. The deeper we dig, the more we see that God does not deviate from His patterns.

So I hope you see that there is a much deeper connection going on here with altars than first thought. All those altars and all those sacrifices throughout time were more than just man's duty to God; they were the very shadow of the Christ to come, as well as the shadow of the relationship of sacrifice between us and God. The altars would be the monuments built by man to aid him in his remembrance of God, much in the same fashion that the cross is a monument for believers today. As Paul said, "For the message of the cross is foolishness to those who are perishing, but to us who are being saved it is the power of God" (1 Corinthians 1:18).

Abraham's altars were a display of the power of God in his life, and this is exactly what Calvary and the cross have become to us today—a display of God's power over sin. Even though it was some two thousand years ago, it still remains a monument to us, a place in time where Christ would go in obedience to God's ordinances, to atone for sin, to appease God's judgments on mankind, and to worship God for His mercy given through this final sacrifice. I know the concept of Christ worshiping upon that cross seems alien to us, but stay with me, and I'll show you later on how it all worked. But through the sacrifice of His body and the pouring out of His blood, Christ made reconciliation for us to God upon the altar of the cross, as Paul said:

> Now all things are of God, who has reconciled us to Himself through Jesus Christ, and has given us the ministry of reconciliation, that is, that God was in Christ reconciling the world to Himself, not imputing their trespasses to them, and has committed to us the word of reconciliation. (2 Corinthians 5:18–19)

Remember God said, "I have given it (the blood of Christ) to you upon the altar (the cross) to make atonement for your souls; for it is the blood that makes atonement for the soul." God was using the events in the life of Abraham and others to systematically fore-shadow the events at Calvary in nearly everything He did. God did not design or inspire anything without Calvary in mind.

You have to keep in mind that the pattern and its forming were in its infancy at this stage. With this relatively new world, He couldn't just come right out of the gate with the Law; it had its time and place as you'll see, but He left us with these very basic shadows to aid us in understanding the rest when it came. You don't just start out in algebra, but you have to learn the basics of math first, 2+2=4, and then you move on—no foundation; no complex math. Just keep following the white rabbit, and you'll soon begin to understand these concepts better. I realize that these descriptions are in their rough form, but as you move along, you'll be able to look back and see all of this very clearly. The more we build on this pattern, the more its solution becomes evident. A+B=C, right?

Isaac

So, with Abraham completing the first portion of the pattern, let's explore Isaac and his contribution to the whole process. We will begin this with the same line of questioning that we did with Abraham. What was Isaac noted for in the Bible besides being the kid that his father almost sacrificed? The answer is digging wells. You see, what might have seemed like an uneventful life in comparison to his father's, especially if you count the pages that were dedicated to each, Isaac nevertheless would become a typesetter through the act of digging wells.

Now, I'm sure for a lot of you, the light just went on when you heard the word well; but let me explain so we can get this out of the way. So how did digging wells shadow the next portion of the pattern, which was the burial of the Christ? Well, I can assure you that it wasn't the actual digging portion, though that could be seen as creating a tomb or digging a grave. No, it is what lay at the bottom of them that God was interested in; and thus, He inspired Isaac to go after that water to create our second symbolic type. So in keeping with the order of the process of Calvary, blood first and then water; this portion was left for Isaac to fulfill.

Now, the Bible steps into Isaac's life rather quickly; in fact, there is only about a chapter and a half that is dedicated to him. So as you can imagine, this will be quick; but after the death of his father Abraham, Isaac began his life by redigging the wells of his father that the Philistines had covered with rocks. When Isaac and his men reopened those wells, they found that the Philistines contested with them on who owned them. I'm sure Isaac was probably thinking, "Then why did you cover them with rocks?" This appears to be that classic of all adages, "We don't want them, but you can't have them, either." So because of their contention, Isaac would eventually move on and dig new wells that would become his own and set our type for the burial. As we tear this story down verse by verse, you'll see that the symbolism is so profoundly acute in Isaacs's case that even in his worship to God, he not only offers a sacrifice but also digs a well. Those wells would serve the same purpose that the flood did with Noah—to shadow the burial of the Christ. So let's explore Isaac and his wells and do a little digging into the allegorical message.

> Then Isaac departed from there and pitched his tent in the Valley of Gerar, and dwelt there. And Isaac **dug again** the wells of **water** which they had dug in the days of Abraham his father, for the Philistines had stopped them up after the death of Abraham. He called them by the names which his father had called them.
>
> Also Isaac's servants dug in the valley, and found a well of running **water** there. But the herdsmen of Gerar quarreled with Isaac's herdsmen, saying, "The water is ours." So he called the name of the well Esek, because they quarreled with him. Then they **dug another well**, and they quarreled over that one also. So he called its name Sitnah. And he moved from there and **dug another well**, and they did not quarrel over it. So he called its name Rehoboth, because he said, "For now the Lord has made room for us, and we shall be fruitful in the land." (Genesis 26:17–22)

So when Isaac reopened his father's wells, the men of the land, the Philistines, fought with them over the water; and when God pressed upon Isaac to move and dig more wells, the herdsmen of that land opposed him on two occasions. So he moved once more and dug new wells; and after three tries, on the fourth one, he found separation from his troubles and room for his flocks and herds. And there again we find the number three in play, for the three times he dug wells before he found the needed separation. It bears the same symbolic meaning as with Abraham and Isaac's three-day journey to the mountain. It was a rebirth for Isaac and his men because there was no more quarreling over water. As I said before, the number three plays a huge part in the building of the pattern because, again, the Christ would remain three days in the tomb. And I know it may appear rough right now for some of you, but stay with me because after you see this same pattern repeated enough times, you will see the formula a little better.

Notice, though, that it wasn't until Isaac repented or turned from the wells of his father and the land of the Philistines, which could be viewed symbolically as living in sin, and dug new wells in a new land that God granted him peace. Isaac had to die out to that former life he knew with his father and forge a new one, thus again modeling the very actions of the Christ and His repentance in the Garden. It's not always easy to turn from what you have known your entire life. And of course you will begin to see this bloodless sacrifice more and more as we move closer to Calvary, because of the actions that the Christ would take in the Garden, turning from His own will and that of God's—first the repentance and turning from self-will, then to the altar, and the blood.

And, as you can imagine, we are not done just yet with Isaac because he goes on to dig a few more wells, and we even find him fulfilling the initial portions of the pattern himself with a sacrifice. Remember that these things build on each other, until they form a complete pattern.

> Then he went up from there to Beersheba. And the Lord appeared to him the same night and said, "I am the God of your father Abraham; do not fear, for I am with you. I will bless you and multiply your descendants for my servant Abraham's sake." So he **built an altar** there and called on the name of the Lord, and he pitched his tent there; **and there Isaac's servants dug a well**. (Verse 23–25)

What I find so amazing about this verse of scripture is just how consistent God is in displaying the elements of His pattern. Like his father before him, we see that when Isaac is visited by God, he builds an altar to honor that visitation and then takes the next step in the process by digging a well. As I said, it is always blood, then water, a death, and then a burial, red and then blue. So we see that the pattern is building with Isaac, working its way to its own resurrection. One more well in the life of Isaac and then we can move on:

> Then Abimelech came to him from Gerar with Ahuzzath, one of his friends, and Phichol the commander of his army. And Isaac said to them, "Why have you come to me, since you hate me and have sent me away from you?" But they said, "We have certainly seen that the Lord is with you." So we said, "Let there now be an oath between us, between you and us; and let us make a covenant with you, that you will do us no harm, since we have not touched you, and since we have done nothing to you but good and have sent you away in peace. You are now the blessed of the Lord." So he made them a feast, and they ate and drank. Then they arose early in the morning and swore an oath with one another; and Isaac sent them away, and they departed from him in peace. It came to pass the same day that Isaac's servants **came and told him about the well which they had dug**, and said to him, "**We have found water**." So he called it Shebah. Therefore the name of the city is Beersheba to this day. (Genesis 26:26–33)

I put the whole event in here because I wanted you to see that after the covenant or contract was sealed with an oath, God showed His approval to Isaac by his servants appearing and pronouncing, "We have found water." As if to make a point with Isaacs's life, God set the exclamation point with one final symbol and a very faint shadow of a resurrection when he is granted peace with his former enemies. And so if you have ever wondered about Isaac digging so many wells, now you know. That's all Isaac's wells were representing—It is the mandated symbolism of the water to act as the tomb of Christ.

And again, it is all very basic if you keep this one concept in mind—follow the blood trail, follow the water trail, and follow the trail of the life changes or miracles. They will lead you to the pattern every time; and, in turn, they will lead us to Calvary. It's all about the symbolism with God; He saw fit to establish the fact that one's faith and His symbolism would work together to saving of His people because faith without the symbolism does nothing for the believer. It leaves you with no path to follow. Also, symbolism without faith is meaningless; they work hand in hand to the saving of God's creation. This is why he left us these symbols—so we could follow them to Calvary.

Jacob

Moving on though, there's one more piece of the puzzle to fit, which is slightly more complicated than those previous. Like Abraham working toward the resurrection, Jacob would have to fulfill the first two portions before he could have his resurrection. You see, when Jacob was born, he was rightly named. Upon coming out of his mother's womb, he was clutching the heel of his twin brother Esau.

> So when her days were fulfilled for her to give birth, indeed there were twins in her womb. And the first came out red. He was like a hairy garment all over; so they called his name Esau. Afterward his brother came out, and his hand took hold of Esau's heel; so his name was called Jacob. (Genesis 25:24–26)

That little stunt of grabbing the heel earned him the name of Jacob, which means "supplanter" or, by definition, "one who wrongfully or illegally seizes and holds the place of another." Remember that names are important.

You see, before they were even born, there was a prophesy that was pronounced to Rebekah. Because she was uncomfortable during her pregnancy, she went to inquire of God as to why she was suffering. She received the prophecy that there were twins fighting in her womb and would continue to fight all their lives, even after they became two separate nations.

> And the children struggled together within her; and she said, "If all is well, why am I like this?" So she went to inquire of the Lord. And the Lord said to her: "Two nations are in your womb, two peoples shall be separated from your body; one people shall be stronger than the other, And the older shall serve the younger. The one people shall be stronger than the other people; and the elder shall serve the younger." (Genesis 25:22–23)

Jacob came out of his mother's womb exactly what God had intended him to be—a supplanter, a man that was conniving and crooked like most, a man so set in his natural ways of deception that only God could change him from that natural deceiver to a spiritual man, from a typical man to a man that has power with God Himself.

Now, I've heard it said that the reason Jacob dealt so treacherously with his brother Esau in stealing his birthright and the blessing of the firstborn was because he desired the spiritual things of God so much that he was willing to do anything. That's a good thought, but it's not accurate. If he was so spiritually minded, then God would have never had to change him. Furthermore, why would he deceive his brother and father in the first place? And, from our readings in the Bible, it appears that God wasn't even on the radar for the first portion of Jacobs's life; moreover, Jacob did not even have his first encounter with God until he fled from the wrath of his brother Esau and stayed the night near the city of Luz, where he received the same promise from God that Abraham and Isaac received.

> Now Jacob went out from Beersheba and went toward Haran. So he came to a certain place and stayed there all night, because the sun had set. And he took one of the stones of that place and put it at his head, and he lay down in that place to sleep. Then he dreamed, and behold, a ladder was set up on the earth, and its top reached to heaven; and there the angels of God were ascending and descending on it. And behold, the Lord stood above it and said: "I am the Lord God of Abraham your father and the God of Isaac; the land on which you lie I will give to you and your descendants. Also your descendants shall be as the dust of the earth; you shall spread abroad to the west and the east, to the north and the south; and in you and in your seed all the families of the earth shall be blessed. Behold, I am with you and will keep you wherever you go, and will bring you back to this land; for I will not leave you **until I have done what I have spoken to you.**" (Genesis 28:10–15)

In essence, until I have completed the pattern.

You see, Jacob wasn't a spiritual man chasing the things of God; he was simply a supplanter running for his life. Again, he was exactly what God wanted him to be—a deceiver, prideful and greedy and willing to do anything to get what he wanted. But the one redeeming quality Jacob had was that he was willing to go the distance to get the things he desired, and God loved that about Jacob. He knew that once He turned him, he would be relentless in going after the will of God. This is why God said later on concerning Jacob and Esau, "Yet Jacob I have loved; But Esau I have hated, and laid waste his mountains and his heritage for the jackals of the wilderness" (Malachi 1:2–3).

Why did He love Jacob and hate Esau, much in the way He had respect for Abel's sacrifice and rejected Cain's? Because Jacob had a drive to succeed. He was a winner, while Esau only cared about the common things in life, just your ordinary average guy. Hunting was more important to him than God, and it always would be.

One more aspect about Jacob not being a man seeking after God was the vow that he entered into with God after his first encounter. If Jacob was truly after the things of God like people think, then I believe the vow he made to God would have sounded a little more committed than what it did:

> Then Jacob made a vow, saying, "**If** God will be with **me**, and keep **me** in this way that **I** am going, and give **me** bread to eat and clothing to put on, so that **I** come back to my father's house in peace, then the Lord shall be my God." (Genesis 28:20–21)

Notice that he opened his vow with an "If," which is known as a conditional clause, a particular stipulation or provision in a contract. This simply meant that this was not going to be a two-way street. As usual, Jacob would do his best to slant the deal in his favor; and if that were not enough, we then see just how selfish Jacob truly was with the remainder of the vow when we see him mention himself some five times in those few words, three of which were "Me" and two "I," culminating finally in the "Proviso" that simply was "**If** God will," "**Then** the Lord shall be mine." This basically meant, do for me first and then I will do for you. So you see, Jacob was not a God-minded man, but a Jacob-minded man, just like the rest of us. Oh, I'm sure he heard stories from his father about the things God had done for his family, but Jacob's come-to-God moment did not happen until he had lied and cheated his way out of his family. As for the vow, that simply displayed Jacob's true nature, which was all right with God, because, again, God had plans for this deceiver.

Now, my point to this tearing down of Jacob's character is that I want you to see the pattern. Jacob was just like his grandfather Abraham before he left Haran and turned to serve God. He was a man of the world, not of God, and he had to be called out of that situation in order for God to paint the allegory. It's important for us to understand just what God would change him from and how this change would fit the pattern. God would have to change Jacob much in the same way Christ was changed from that physical man that died on the cross into the man that could suddenly appear in a room with his wounds still evident. As John testified of:

> And after eight days His disciples were again inside, and Thomas with them. Jesus came, the doors being shut, and stood in the midst, and said, "Peace to you!" Then He said to Thomas, "Reach your finger here, and look at my hands; and reach your hand here, and put it into my side. Do not be unbelieving, but believing." (John 20:26–27)

So you see, where the Christ would be physically transfigured or changed after His resurrection, Jacob would have to be symbolically transfigured in a spiritual sense after his resurrection, changed from this deceiver to a man that would have power with both God and men, just as the Christ would. And this is entirely indicative of our relationship with God today—We ourselves must all take part in this transfiguration, moving from the land of the dead to the land of the living, just as Jacob and the Christ did.

Now, in Jacobs's first encounter with God, we see that he built a stone altar much like his great-grandfather did after his encounters; but instead of sacrificing an animal upon it and shedding blood, he poured oil on it. Why the change? Because, if you remember, he was a man on the run from his brother. He was not traveling with flocks and herds of animals that would have provided an available sacrifice. Besides, seeing the haste in which he left, I'm sure he was traveling quite light.

> And the words of Esau her older son, were told to Rebekah. So she sent and called Jacob her younger son, and said to him, "Surely your brother Esau comforts himself concerning you by intending to kill you. Now therefore, my son, obey my voice: arise, flee to my brother Laban in Haran." (Genesis 27:42–43)

So considering the situation, the oil was probably the most costly possession he had. He simply made do and sacrificed from those apparently limited means. And interestingly enough, God honored the sacrifice because it was still seen as something that cost Jacob something of value. The oil acted the same as the blood; it would, in essence, become the accepted payment that was used to seal the contract or vow between him and God and the first symbolic step in completing the pattern of Calvary in his life. Now, we just have to look for the second elemental portion of the pattern, which would be fulfilled when he first meets Rachel:

> So Jacob went on his journey and came to the land of the people of the East. And he looked, and saw a **well** in the field; and behold, there were three flocks of sheep lying by it; for out of that well they **watered** the flocks. A large stone was on the well's mouth. Now all the flocks would be gathered there; and they would roll the stone from the well's mouth, water the sheep, and put the stone back in its place on the well's mouth.
>
> And Jacob said to them, "My brethren, where are you from?" And they said, "We are from Haran." Then he said to them, "Do you know Laban the son of Nahor?" And they said, "We know him." So he said to them, "Is he well?" And they said, "He is well. And look, his daughter Rachel is coming with the sheep." Then he said, "Look, it is still high day; it is not time

for the cattle to be gathered together. Water the sheep, and go and feed them." But they said, "We cannot until all the flocks are gathered together, and they have rolled the stone from the well's mouth; then we water the sheep." Now while he was still speaking with them, Rachel came with her father's sheep, for she was a shepherdess. And it came to pass, when Jacob saw Rachel the daughter of Laban his mother's brother, and the sheep of Laban his mother's brother, that Jacob went near and **rolled the stone from the well's mouth, and watered the flock** of Laban his mother's brother. (Genesis 29:1–10)

So was it a coincidence that the next incident in Jacob's life involved a well, or was it by design? And was it the inspiration of God that also caused Rachel to come out just at that time of the day, when it wasn't even the proper time to water the sheep, or just another coincidence? No, it was not; as usual, we see that God is orchestrating events in the lives of the people that He is using. God drew them both there at that precise time so that Jacob could fulfill the second elemental portion of the pattern with that water from the well. You do realize that Jacob could have just walked straight into the city of Haran, right? But, if you don't believe me, remember that God told Jacob, "For I will not leave you until I have done what I have spoken to you." God was with Jacob, fulfilling His portion of the contract, leading Jacob in the building of the pattern. And again, as we have seen before with these patterns, God was adding little nuances to its design as each pattern developed. Because you see, this little event went even deeper than what it appears to be on the surface. This little allegory would also shadow an event on resurrection morning when Jesus would rise from the actual tomb.

Now after the Sabbath, as the first day of the week began to dawn, Mary Magdalene and the other Mary came to see the tomb. And behold, there was a great earthquake; for an angel of the Lord descended from heaven, and came and **rolled back the stone from the door**, and sat on it. His countenance was like lightning and his clothing as white as snow. And the guards shook for fear of him, and became like dead men. (Matthew 28:1–4)

Again, in a very faint shadow, God adds a small but significant element to the allegory by Jacob rolling the stone away for Rachel and allowing the water to flow from the well. In that act, God simply and subtly foreshadowed that event when the stone would be rolled away from the tomb of the Christ, thus allowing Jesus, the living waters, as He described Himself, to flow into a dry and thirsty world and water the flocks of God.

I know it may seem like reaching to some at this point in the story, but this rock was no different than the rib of Adam; God was simply foreshadowing a future event. We need to keep in mind that the pattern was in its infancy here, in its early cellular development; no one was going to get anything complex at this stage. Again, that was not going to happen until the Tabernacle was built and the Law was given. So what may seem vague and reaching in your understanding is really only because the complexity of the pattern was building. These are the simple and modest foundations; it is from these origins that we begin to build the house of Calvary.

But in that subtle display is the very nature of God—to take something as simple as water and a stone and turn it into a divine allegorical meaning. I believe that's partly why water's true meaning has never been clearly understood. It is used in so many different ways that it made it hard for us to pin it down. It is a flood here and a river crossing there and even something so simple as rolling a stone away from over the mouth of a well. In fact, it has taken me several years to fully comprehend the vastness of its meanings and uses. Again, this was done in such a way because God could not convey this layered meaning in just one event.

And trust me, I know; it's surprisingly easy to pass over all these the little phrases and nuances of the Bible; but it is because we never really understood what was going on; and we really had no clue what we were looking for. And, in reality, we had no reason to look; we thought we understood it all. And unfortunately, the things we could not understand, we simply dismissed. This brings to mind a portion of the Kolbrin Bible I like to quote that says:

> Yet man is man, and ever fated to search out beyond himself, striving to attain things which always just elude his grasp. So in his frustration he replaces the dimly seen incomprehensible with things that are with in his understanding. If these things but poorly reflect reality, distorted though it may be, of great value than no reflection at all.

What the writer is saying there is that it is in man's nature to find something to fit into things that he does not understand, even if it doesn't make sense. He does it because he would rather have a half-truth than nothing at all.

But when you know what it is all about, when you know that Calvary was on the forefront of God's mind, it is at that point that one begins to see how God was thinking. You begin to see God building this amazing image of what was to be Calvary in the seemingly everyday ordinary events and lives of the people that we have always heard about, but again, we never really understood. The pattern is sort of the Rosetta stone of the Bible because it makes these seemingly insignificant things significant, deciphering the once indecipherable.

Turning our attention back to the story of Jacob, we now find him living with his uncle Laban, a man who was just like him, a deceiver; it's almost amusing to see Jacob repaid for the things he had done to his father and brother by his own flesh and blood. It always seems like God has a way of balancing out the scales; it is divine justice, or karma if you prefer. I believe it was the Norse men that said it best, "Wyrd bið ful aræd" or "Fate is inexorable." Jacob could not escape, nor change his fate, even if he was smart enough to know what was about to happen to him. Because you see, while he was living on the run with Laban, Jacob made a vow with him also, to serve him for seven years in return for Rachel's hand in marriage.

> Now Jacob loved Rachel; so he said, "I will serve you seven years for Rachel your younger daughter." And Laban said, "It is better that I give her to you than that I should give her to another man. Stay with me." So Jacob served seven years for Rachel, and they seemed only a few days to him because of the love he had for her. Then Jacob said to Laban, "Give me my wife, for my days are fulfilled, that I may go in to her." And Laban gathered together all the men of the place and made a feast. Now it came to pass in the evening that he took Leah his daughter and brought her to Jacob; and he went in to her. And Laban gave his maid Zilpah to his daughter Leah as a maid. So it came to pass in the morning, that behold, it was Leah. And he said to Laban, "What is this you have done to me? Was it not for Rachel that I served you? **Why then have you deceived me?"** And Laban said, "It must not be done so in our country, to give the younger before the firstborn. Fulfill her week, and we will give you this one also for the service which you will serve with me still another seven years." (Genesis 29:18–27)

Paying your debt to society or God is a bitter experience; trust me, I know firsthand on both accounts. So I somewhat sympathize with Jacob, but it is also good to see a deceitful person get a taste of their own medicine. Jacob found out he didn't like it, but God wasn't done with him just yet. There was a large debt against Jacob on the scales of justice that needed to be paid, just like each and every one of us. It is nice to know, though, that God always balances out those scales of justice for the ones He loves.

Now, stay with me on this next part, it may seem like nothing; but again, we are establishing the character of Jacob in order to show you just how much God would change him. So after Jacob served the additional seven years for Rachel, God began to bless Jacob and make him a great man, even while balancing out those scales. And even though Jacob seemed done with his deceptions, his new father-in-law Laban was not. I really think it was God causing Laban to deceive Jacob in order to push him out of his comfort zone and back to the land of promise and the final confrontation with his brother Esau. So after serving Laban for over twenty years and being deceived multiple times, Jacob had finally had enough. It was time to leave, but because he feared Laban and his sons, he decided to flee while his father-in-law was out of town.

Now, I will spare you the lengthy story and simply tell you that God instructed Jacob to return home to his father's house; and, out of fear of Laban, he decides to disembark while Laban was out shearing the sheep. By the time the news arrives to Laban, three days had already gone by, and it takes another seven days for Laban to catch up with Jacob and his caravan.

> And Jacob stole away, unknown to Laban the Syrian, in that he did not tell him that he intended to flee. So he fled with all that he had. He arose and crossed the river, and headed toward the mountains of Gilead. And Laban was told on the **third** day that Jacob had fled. Then he took his brethren with him and pursued him for seven days' journey, and he overtook him in the mountains of Gilead. (Genesis 31:20–23)

So the night before the confrontation, God appears to Laban in a dream and tells him, "Be careful that you speak to Jacob neither good nor bad" (verse 24); and so Laban does as he is told the next day. Now, upon a brief chastising from Laban and a thorough searching of his caravan for his stolen idols that his daughter Rachel took, Jacob and Laban agree to make a covenant.

Then Laban said to Jacob, "Here is this heap and here is this pillar, which I have placed between you and me. This heap is a witness, and this pillar is a witness that I will not pass beyond this heap to you, and you will not pass beyond this heap and this pillar to me, for harm. The God of Abraham, the God of Nahor, and the God of their father judge between us." And Jacob swore by the Fear of his father Isaac. Then Jacob **offered a sacrifice** on the mountain, and called his brethren to eat bread. And they ate bread and stayed all night on the mountain. And early in the morning Laban arose, and kissed his sons and daughters and blessed them. Then Laban departed and returned to his place. (Genesis 31:51–55)

So as you can imagine, there was more to this little story of escape than first thought. For starters, the numbers three and seven should have jumped out at you from our number lesson before. And the fact that there was an evident sacrifice committed should draw your attention as well. But the real question is, of course, what did they mean in this context? Well, those first three days of flight, before Laban was notified, were, of course, a very faint shadow of the burial term of the Christ. And so compound that with Abraham and Isaac's three-day journey, and now we begin to see a bit of a pattern beginning to develop.

So those three days of unknown flight served as a sort of covering, a burial if you will; it was a time where Laban had no clue that Jacob had stolen away. But it was at that third-day point when he became aware that Jacob had truly broken free from his bondage, that Jacob would fulfill the symbolic shadow of the resurrection, entering into a truly born again moment, leaving his life of servitude and entering into his wilderness journey back to the Promised Land. This dovetails nicely into the events of Calvary because, after those three days in the tomb, it became apparent that the Christ had escaped His bondage of death and was now free to return home to heaven after a brief forty-day stay in that wilderness between heaven and earth.

And this is a good example of how, once you know what to look for and how the process works, you can then plug in the story around those patterns until they fit Calvary. So understanding what three really was designed to be in biblical terms, it's easy to see that those three days of unknown flight symbolically fit the burial term of the Christ and His subsequent resurrection. And it's important here to see that in Jacobs's decision to repent, or turn, from serving Laban and return to the land of his fathers, he was symbolically dying to that former life, just as the Christ would die out to His former life while praying in the garden of Gethsemane, when He said, "Father, if you are willing, take this cup from me; yet **not my will**, **but yours** be done" (Luke 22:42).

Furthermore, we see that Jacob had unknowingly mimicked the same form of repentance that his father Isaac and grandfather Abraham had performed years earlier—first, when Abraham had repented from the same country of Haran, where Jacob was now serving Laban, and secondly, when his father Isaac had finally had enough of fighting over the wells with the Philistines and he turned and removed himself from that land to another,

> And he moved from there and dug another well,
> and they did not quarrel over it. So he called its
> name Rehoboth, because he said, "For now the
> Lord has made room for us, and we shall be fruit-
> ful in the land." (Genesis 26:22).

The other predictable portion of this pattern was that after Jacob repented or turned from serving Laban, notice that he crossed the river, "He arose and crossed the river, and headed toward the mountains of Gilead." Which of course would have been the same river that his grandfather Abraham crossed to begin his journey some years previous. Thus symbolically, Jacob entered into the burial of Christ and that three day term. As for the seven days, that, of course, is the number of completion and rest. When Laban finally did catch up with Jacob, it was too late. God had intervened in a dream on his behalf and thus completed Jacob's escape; he could finally rest from the fear and servitude of Laban. So, to summarize, we have Jacob dying out to that former life and then crosses the river, which then symbolically buried or hid Jacob for those three days of flight. Then, there is a very faint resurrection when Laban is forced by God to let Jacob go, much in the same way God would force the grave to let the Christ go. Now, if you noticed, God is developing two patterns within the same story, one of which is very symbolic like this one and then one will be entirely physical, using actual blood and water and the evident change. Why? Because the Christ would first come and fulfill those symbolic requirements when He was baptized in the Jordan, and then, He would go to Calvary and fulfill all the physical requirements.

As I have said before, it's always patterns inside of patterns; even though some are very subtle, they still represent the whole of Calvary, which makes the Bible highly predictable once you know what you are looking for. And as usual, while building one pattern, God sets up the beginning of the next one, which was when Jacob would make that sacrifice upon the mountain. And so we step into the next and final portion of the pattern.

Now, Jacob knew that his returning home was going to be a problem because of his underhanded dealings with his brother Esau, who, remember, swore in his heart that he would kill Jacob for stealing his birthright. So, being unsure of just how to approach Esau, and if time had even healed those wounds, Jacob decides to send messengers to Esau to announce his return and to test the waters. The response he received was less than favorable when the messenger tells him, "We came to your brother Esau, and he also is coming to meet you, and four hundred men are with him. So Jacob was greatly afraid and distressed" (Genesis 32:6).

And as the story goes, Jacob devises a plan to send a peace offering before him in waves, so that if Esau attacked the first wave, the rest could get away. Now, keep in mind that this was a designed response that was inspired by God to push Jacob into fulfilling the next portion of the pattern. As we now see Jacob taking those first steps by praying to God to deliver him, "Deliver me, I pray, from the hand of my brother, from the hand of Esau; for I fear him, lest he come and attack me and the mother with the children" (Genesis 32:11). This was the breaking point for Jacob, the place where God had always wanted him, trapped between that proverbial rock and a hard place, a place of sheer desperation where Jacob could no longer rely on his own cunning, but had to turn to God, unknowingly setting the stage for the final portions of the pattern.

> And he arose that night and took his **two** wives, his **two** female servants, and his **eleven** sons, and **crossed over the ford of Jabbok**. He took them, sent them over the brook, and sent over what he had. Then Jacob was left alone; and a Man wrestled with him until the breaking of day. Now when he saw that he did not prevail against him, he touched the socket of his hip; and the socket of Jacob's hip was out of joint as he wrestled with him. And he said, "Let Me go, for the day breaks." But he said, "**I will not let you go unless you bless me!**" So he said to him, "**What is your name**?" He said, "**Jacob**." And he said, "Your name shall no longer be called Jacob, **but Israel**; for you have struggled with God and with men, and have prevailed." Then Jacob asked, saying, "Tell me your name, I pray." And he said, "Why is it that you ask about my name?" And he blessed him there." (Genesis 32:22–29)

So was it a surprise to see that Jacob's next move involved water, especially after seeing that he sacrificed on the mountain after the meeting with Laban? Probably not, but that's because in just a few chapters, we have already begun to see the predictability of the pattern. And that's what I meant by following the blood trail. It always leads you to the water, and the water leads you to the miraculous. So Jacob arose that night and took his family across the brook Jabbok.

Notice that the Bible said that he crossed over with his two wives and their two servants and his eleven sons. Now, I have a theory on this, but we will explore that a little later.

Now if you didn't catch this little action in the verse, what happens is that Jacob makes the decision to send his family back across the brook, so that he is left alone to face this insurmountable problem, as if to suggest, "I have run long enough; it's time to face God and my problems." And once alone, he finds himself wrestling with what the Bible calls a man, and what most have called an angel, but what Jacob called God. And this goes on until daybreak, when the man finally says, "Let me go." In his desperation, Jacob refuses to let go until he receives the thing he is after—a blessing to be at peace with his brother. Thus, he says, "I will not let you go unless you bless me!" As I said before, God loved Jacob for his tenacity; his willingness to go the distance was much like that of the Christ, and I believe that's why God molded Jacob's life in such a way. This was all so that we would have a better understanding of the struggles that the Christ would go through one day on His journey to the Father.

And so God blessed Jacob; but if you will notice, just before the blessing is conveyed, the man asks him, "What is your name?" That's an interesting question to ask someone that you have been literally fighting with, especially seeing that he just ruined your hip forever. So why did he ask Jacob his name, when apparently this was, at the very least, some sort of divine creature that he was struggling with? I mean, it is a given that he would have known his name, right? He did that to force Jacob to understand who he was, who he had always been—a deceiver—as if to make Jacob recall his entire life up to this point and to emphasize what was about to be changed in his life when He would bestow the blessing upon him: "Your name shall no longer be called Jacob, but Israel; for you have struggled with God and with men, and have prevailed."

So, within the context of those few verses, we see that Jacob fulfills the last two portions of the pattern—first, by crossing over the brook Jabbok to symbolize the burial of the Christ because when Jacob crossed the brook the first time, he was, in a very literal sense, a dead man. Esau was going to kill him and he knew it; that's why crossing that brook would be a perfect symbol of the Christ being placed in the tomb. And when that epic struggle began on the other side of the river, it was to foreshadow the battle that would occur between the Christ and Lucifer for the "keys of Death and Hell"; only Jacob's struggle was for the keys to his physical salvation.

And of course, after receiving the blessing, Jacob crossed the brook for the final time as Israel, a completely changed and resurrected man from that former life. He was truly born again, a changed man in every way. So not only did he have his name and his deceitful nature changed, but also the outcome of his encounter with Esau was changed. The life of Jacob and his transformation were one of the most symbolically complete reflections of the resurrection in the Bible. That is exactly what the resurrection would be for the Christ—a transformation from a man bound by the flesh and its weakness to a man that was free from the constraints of mortality, free from the fear that He had displayed in the Garden. In essence, the Christ went to His death a symbolic Jacob, weak in the flesh, but was resurrected a very literal Israel because He had struggled with God and His own will in the Garden, struggled with man His entire ministry, and prevailed when He was resurrected: "for you have struggled with God and with men, and have prevailed." (Genesis 32:28)

So, when Jacob crossed the brook for the final time as Israel to face his brother, he found that Esau no longer wanted to kill him: "But Esau ran to meet him, and embraced him, and fell on his neck and kissed him, and they wept" (Genesis 33:4). The last few hours of Jacob's life simply astonished me in how much they paralleled that of the Christ and His final hours. These last few verse paints such a vivid picture for us, though symbolic, of the burial and resurrection of the Christ and His unseen struggle for those keys. When I read of Jacob's struggle, I can't help but recall that prophesy that was made in the Garden of Eden when the Lord said, "He will crush your head, and you will strike his heel." Like Jacob, the Christ would not come out of that battle unscathed, seeing that He paid with his life rather than His hip, but in his resurrection, He crushed the head of death, hell, and the grave.

And here is an interesting little side note; remember that I said I had a theory about the eleven sons of Jacob crossing the brook with him? Well, that number just so happens to be the exact number of disciples that Jesus entered the garden of Gethsemane with in His hour of tribulation because if you are familiar with the story, you will remember that Judas had left the upper room earlier to betray the Christ. But what's interesting about the whole thing is that it appears that this was the message that God was trying transmit. Jacob, in his hour of distress, not knowing if he was going to live or die, crossed over that brook with his eleven sons; and just as Jesus had removed Himself further from His disciples while in the garden to pray, "Then Jesus came with them to a place called Gethsemane, and said to the disciples, "Sit here while I go and pray over there" (Matthew 26:36). So, too, did Jacob, by sending his family back across the brook so that he could pray and wrestle with that man.

And there is another interesting parallel to the story; it is when Jacob was locked in that intense struggle for the blessing. That event appears to parallel the intensity that the Christ would pray with in the garden, almost wrestling with Himself for His very freedom from what was about to happen, as Luke records, "And being in agony, He prayed more earnestly. Then His sweat became like great drops of **blood** falling down to the ground" (verse 22:44). I could not imagine the amount of pressure that one would have to be under to pray until you sweat blood, but I suppose at that moment, He was like Atlas, literally bearing the weight of the world on His shoulders.

Now, I only mention this because the similarities between the two caught my attention, but the thing that troubles me about this thought is that it doesn't fit into the sequence of events. Remember that Jesus prayed first, then was crucified, and buried. It's all about perspective and context, and it is when people take things out of their proper context that falsehoods run rampant. But it really does look like that was the message that God was trying to transmit despite the sequence. Now, the way I have generally viewed it has been that Jacob's wrestling with that man was a symbolic foreshadowing that the Christ, after His burial, would be locked in a struggle with Lucifer, as already mentioned. But I suppose it could be seen as looking at both sides of the coin.

So in closing, I hope it's at least a little easier to see why God said that He was the God of Abraham, Isaac, and Jacob, especially when you take the stories at face value. Without the probing, Abraham's story simply relates his sacrifices, and Isaacs relates his digging of wells, and Jacob's relates to his transformation or resurrection. And that is what makes their story so unique in the Bible. Instead of God building the pattern in one story or one life, He built the pattern over the course of three generations. Therefore, when He says, "I am the God of Abraham, Isaac and Jacob," what He is really saying is, "I am the God of the death, burial and resurrection," or "I am the God of the blood, water and the miraculous," or you could condense it and say "I am the God of Calvary." It kind of lends a new twist to the whole "I am that I am" concept; He is, as they say, all sufficient.

The whole process simply amazes me. God displays His patterns so subtly, hiding them in among the lives and the stories of the Bible, all the while managing to keep them simple and quite beautiful. God's designs are so easy to see once you know what you're looking for, because His mind was always on Calvary. We've only begun to scratch the surface of God's pattern and just how deep it really goes, but by the end of the series, you'll see how ingrained this pattern is throughout the Bible. Into every word and action, God had something in mind.

> All things are hidden, obscure and debatable if the cause of the phenomena is unknown, but everything is clear if the cause be known. (Louis Pasteur)